THIS BOOK BELONGS TO

FOR THE LOVE OF OLD

First published in the
United States of America in 2006
By Rizzoli International Publishing
300 Park Avenue South
New York, NY 10010
www.rizzoliusa.com

© Mary Randolph Carter
© Rizzoli International Publications, Inc.

Design by Aoife Wasser

Poem on page 41, *On the Roof of the World* by Michael
Dennis Browne, reprinted with the permission of the
author.

2006 2007 2008 2009 / 10 9 8 7 6 5 4 3 2 1

ISBN-10: 0-8478-2847-6
ISBN-13: 978-0-8478-2847-0

Library of Congress Control Number: 2006930957

Printed in the United States of America

FOR THE LOVE OF OLD

LIVING WITH CHIPPED, FRAYED, TARNISHED,
FADED, TATTERED, WORN, AND WEATHERED THINGS
THAT BRING COMFORT, CHARACTER, AND JOY
TO THE PLACES WE CALL HOME

WRITTEN AND PHOTOGRAPHED
BY MARY RANDOLPH CARTER

RIZZOLI
NEW YORK

DEDICATION

FOR MY FATHER

With a turn of that old key

You opened the door to my heart

to love worn and weathered things.

beams and bricks,

hinges, nails, maps,

aged houses and fences,

the glint of gold from the worn-down crest on your signet ring.

CONTENTS

INTRODUCTION

Old books,
clothes,
cars,
music,
furniture,
chairs,
tables,
surfaces,
fabrics,
houses,
stories,
movies,
churches,
hymns,
prayers,
people.

EVERYTHING I LOVE IS OLD

My wedding ring came from a secondhand shop.
So did my favorite boots, clothes, books, and paintings.
I love things that are worn (or have been worn) and weathered.

I love rusty
chipped,
frayed,
mended,
mossy,
cracked,
faded,
patched,
peeling,
scuffed
and
faded things.

I have always loved old walls etched with character like the lined face of Georgia O'Keeffe. I will never scrape the pockmarked paint from the front door of our two-hundred-year-old house in the country. I prefer keys, hinges that are rusty, pewter dulled and dented by time, family photographs faded to delicate sepia tones, paintings artfully distressed in chipped gilt frames or frameless, old floorboards that creak underfoot and shine under threadbare carpets, fragile paper lanterns, garden sculptures weathered by summer storms and windy days, venerable armchairs and sofas covered with timeworn fabrics, tables set with handed-down china and monogrammed silver, windows and window seats cozied by thick curtains, old mantles sheltering the warmth of a glowing fire, and piles of old books and frayed pillows scattered everywhere. I love things like these that warm our homes because they warm our hearts.

MUSKETTOE POINTE FARM, CIRCA 1700, BEFORE ITS RESTORATION BEGAN IN 1962.

I am either doomed or blessed to have chosen to live with
things that show their age in places that have resisted the
test of time. In the pages to come, three of these places
are the backdrop and inspiration for this celebration of
the qualities of old. Foremost among them is Muskettoe
Pointe Farm, my family's seventeenth-century home in
the Tidewater area of Virginia. Then, there is Elm Glen
Farm, an old New England-style farmhouse, circa 1800,
nestled in the foothills of the Berkshires in upstate New
York that has been a refuge for me, my husband, and two
sons for almost twenty years. And, finally, there is the
apartment twelve stories up in New York City, which has

ELM GLEN FARM, CIRCA 1800, A WEATHERED BEAUTY IN 1926.

been our nest for three decades. Think of them as stand-ins for the places we all call home, whether old or new, skyscraper or cottage, with a view of rivers, forests, hills, or high-rises, in the north, south, east, or west. Where we live is less the point than how we live and the environments we create to comfort us, our family, and friends.

In an era that is desperate to be young and new and hip and cool, I choose old. This book is not an apology nor a revolt, but a celebration of things that endure, not only the worn and weathered things in our houses, but those of the heart, including love, emotion, character, and integrity. This book, then, is for the love of old.

TARNISHED

It doesn't take long for a piece of silver to show signs of tarnish. Warm weather contributes to that, and moist air, which is why it's a good thing to store it in dark boxes or seal it in airtight baggies. When my husband and I were married, we were given a dozen silver place settings from my family. For most of the year, until Thanksgiving or some very special celebration, it remains stowed away in a drawer in our kitchen. For everyday, we set our table with a mixed set of forks, knives, and spoons collected from tag-sale tables and flea markets. I don't know why we don't use our silver every day. If we did, we wouldn't have to polish it as often, and we'd get to enjoy it more.

Pewter is a family tradition that was started by my father about four decades ago, after we moved into Muskettoe Pointe Farm, an early Virginia farmhouse on the shores of the Rappahannock River and the Chesapeake Bay. It not only suited the period of the house, it suited our big family as well. There were eleven of us—my parents, seven daughters, and two sons—plus (always at mealtime it seemed) an overflow of extra friends and family. Pewter is pretty indestructible, requires no polishing, and the more we used it, banged it, scraped it with spoons and knives, even inadvertently shoved it into the dishwasher, it just got better and older looking!

Opposite: This pewter dinner plate looks older than its years after four decades of family meals. Collect old pewter to display, but for everyday use opt for something new. The lead in antique pewter is what gives it its wonderful dark color, but it's also why you don't want to quaff a beer from an old pewter tankard or eat off an old pewter plate. Modern pewter is lead-free and in time, without treating it too carefully, can look like the real thing!

Don't hide your collections of silver and pewter behind closed doors. Display them openly, even though they may tarnish more quickly. Mix old and new, pewter and silver, tankards and trophies all together. Choose a glassfront cupboard or simple open shelves like the tall skinny set, seen at right, built into a corner of the kitchen at Muskettoe Pointe Farm. Although the original structure is supposedly more than three hundred years old, the current kitchen was added only about forty years ago—something you'd never guess given my parents' choice of old materials, like the wood of these shelves, and the old blue-green paint stroked on behind them,

giving each piece more prominence. The shelves are now a catch-all for a mismatched family of silver and pewter. Starting at the top are a collection of retired pitchers and tankards, which for one reason or another—they leak, or are corroded—can't perform their former duties, but occasionally are called back to stand in as vases for dried herbs and such. Below them on the right are our stacked-up Jefferson cups and to the left various pewter tankards and a pair of salt and pepper shakers. Below that is assorted drinking gear, and to the right is my mother's cache of girlhood trophies. The bottom shelf holds a silver epergne with cake knives and bone-handled cutlery.

Above left: I find pouring water, lemonade, milk, or even a batch of rum punch from a pitcher, particularly a distinguished old pitcher, an old-fashioned pleasure. It's like hanging fresh laundry on a clothesline or cutting flowers from your own garden. Battered but beautiful, this modern pewter specimen has filled many a Jefferson cup, and when it ends up like many of our old pitchers with a leak in

a seam or a hole in its bottom, we will retire it to an unreachable shelf, such as the one at right, along with a legion of other decrepit and world-wearied old soldiers of the home. (Most antique pewter contains lead, so beware of drinking, pouring, or eating off of the real thing!)

Above right: Cherish your trophies and those of your children whether they be

silver, paper, or plastic. One day they will provoke the same kind of memories as my mother's silver loving cup, which was awarded her when she was a junior counselor at Camp Okahawis. Over the years each of us children, and now her grandchildren and great-grandchildren, has removed it carefully from her trophy shelf and sought her out to hear the stories that rise up out of it like those told around a campfire.

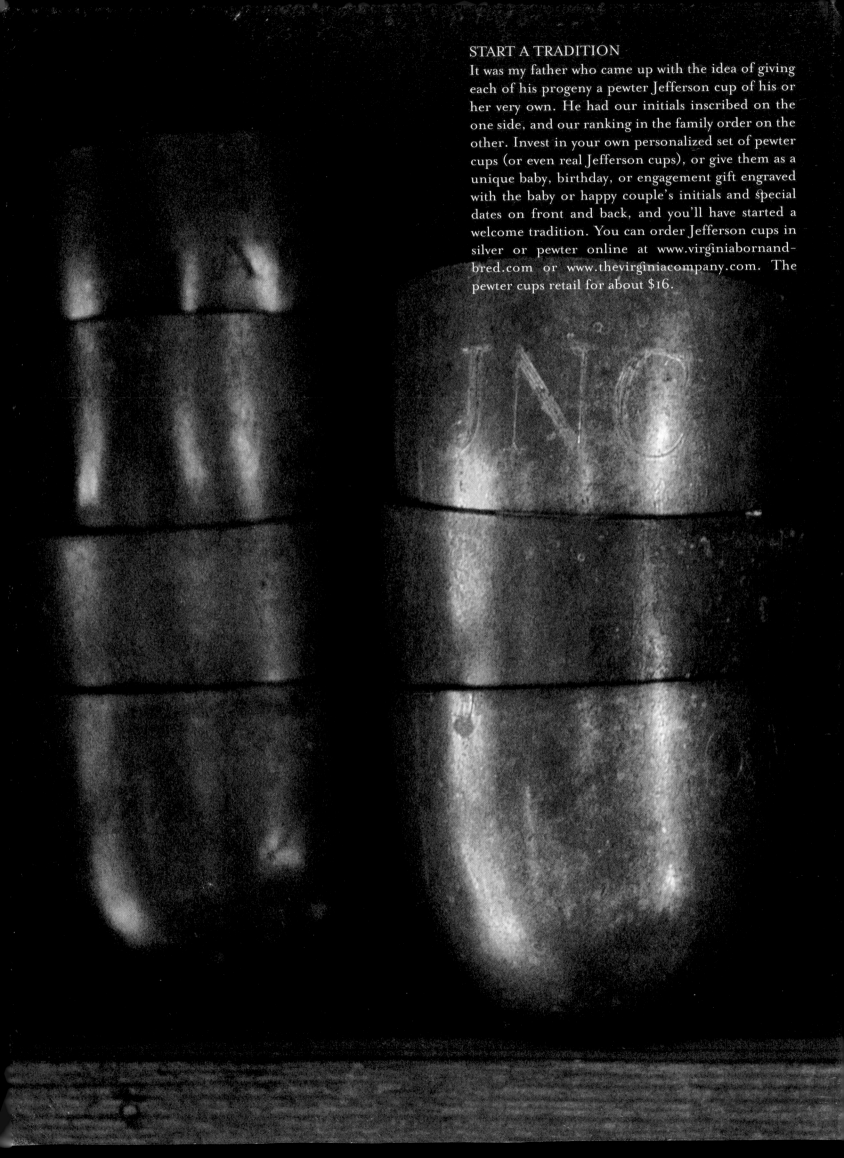

START A TRADITION

It was my father who came up with the idea of giving each of his progeny a pewter Jefferson cup of his or her very own. He had our initials inscribed on the one side, and our ranking in the family order on the other. Invest in your own personalized set of pewter cups (or even real Jefferson cups), or give them as a unique baby, birthday, or engagement gift engraved with the baby or happy couple's initials and special dates on front and back, and you'll have started a welcome tradition. You can order Jefferson cups in silver or pewter online at www.virginiabornand-bred.com or www.thevirginiacompany.com. The pewter cups retail for about $16.

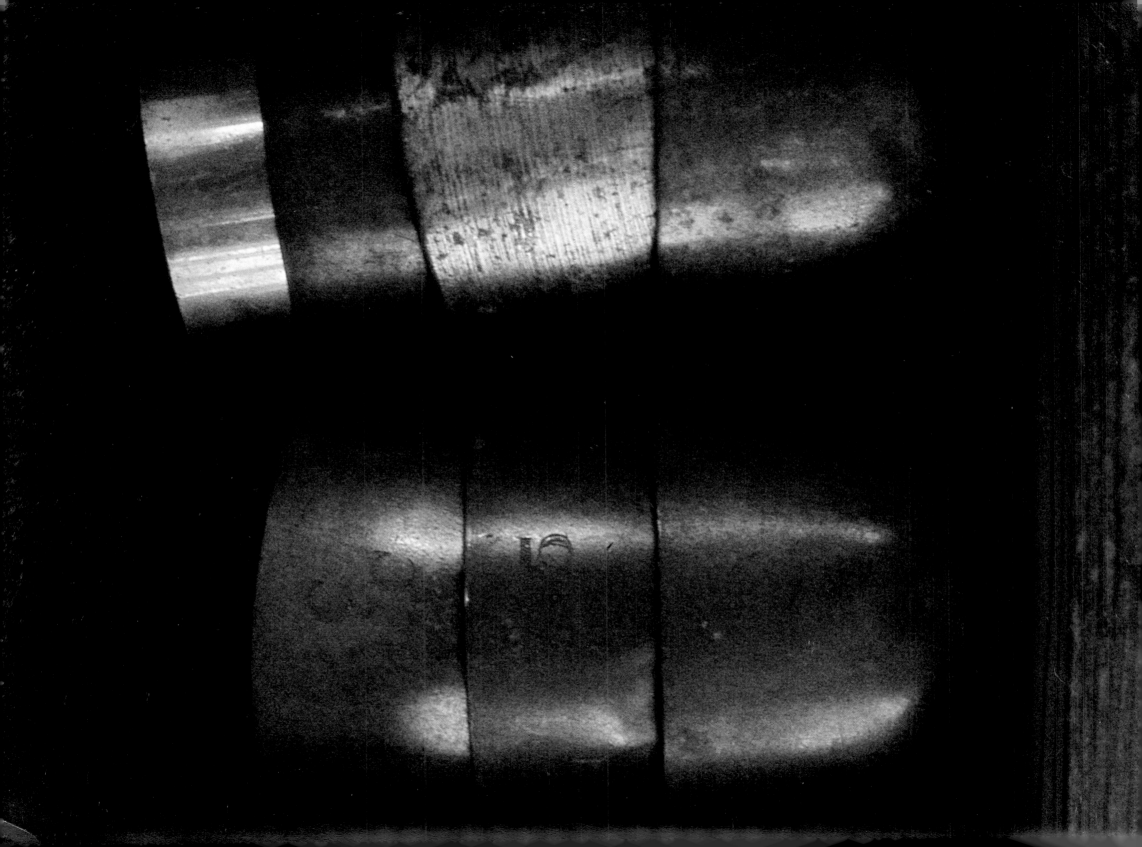

A Tarnished Tale

If my Aunt Nancy had owned pewter instead of silver, she never would have had to worry about polishing it (if she ever did have such a worry!), and I would have neither this untarnished memory of her nor of the chocolate cake she made that day.

I never called my mother's sister "Aunt" Nancy, only Nancy. My cousin Betsey was my best childhood friend, so we took turns spending nights at each other's houses. One Saturday Betsey and I noticed that her mother's silver service, on display in the dining room, had turned black. We decided to do it for her, and with the help of lots of creamy pink silver polish, we took on the task. Although it took us at least two hours to clean up the six pieces and the large tray, I remember how incredibly beautiful the transformation was and how satisfying it was to rub off all the tarnish to reveal the beauty of the silver underneath. When Nancy came home, Betsey and I made her close her eyes, and dragged her to stand in front of the gleaming silver service. "Open your eyes," we instructed, and when she did she gasped and gave us big hugs, and later she baked us one of her special chocolate cakes. Looking back, I wonder if Nancy was really happy with our handiwork or if she, like me today, preferred her silver tarnished!

Let me state from the start that my love of old things certainly includes a love of old silver. But, do I love it more than pewter? Well, absolutely not!

I have heard from friends who grew up with old family silver their fond memories of sitting around the kitchen table sharing a bottle of pink silver cream and polishing cloths torn from old white sheets. There are tales of certain sterling pieces handed down from great-grandmothers and aunts, and others with ancient hallmarks pressed into their backs suggesting their worth, and a visit to *The Antiques Roadshow*. When the task is completed and all the silver is rinsed and dried and softly polished in preparation for whatever family event is to follow, there are sighs of satisfaction that this is a noble task well done. Later, when these pieces are set on a table covered in white damask mixed with other collections of family china, crystal, and the like, there is a reverence for the day and the gathering and the family members—past and present—who follow this tradition.

So, for you silver lovers, some home truths that I respect, but don't always live by . . .

⊘ Most of all, use your silver, and when you are through gently wash it with a phosphate-free detergent.

⊘ Silver that is stored properly is almost tarnish-proof. If you're putting silver away for a hibernation of sorts, wrap each piece in a non-buffered tissue paper or anti-tarnish tissue and seal in a ziploc bag or in flannel rolls or in a specially lined silver box. For everyday use, store in a drawer that's free from moisture. Do not use plastic wrap, newspaper, or rubber bands.

⊘ Sulfides are the enemy! Eggs, fruit juices, vinegar, salty foods, mustard, salad dressings, to name a few, will turn silver green.

⊘ Early tarnish is easily removed, but when it turns black it is much more difficult and requires more abrasive cleansers.

⊘ Apply your silver cream with a damp cellulose sponge—"just a dab'll do ya." Always use a clean, soft cotton cloth—old holey sheets that are soft but no longer bed-acceptable are the ultimate polishing cloth.

⊘ Rub the silver piece in a uniform manner—up and down, never in a circular motion.

⊘ Do not put silver in the dishwasher. It can turn your silver a strange color, loosen knife blades, and strip the silver of its reflective surface. And, never use those silver dips as they can remove all authentic patina.

⊘ Forget those tips about cleaning silver with toothpaste.

⊘ Don't use dried-up polishes or a scouring pad.

⊘ Or consider the alternative to all of this—switch to pewter! The pieces at right are still shiny after three decades of use.

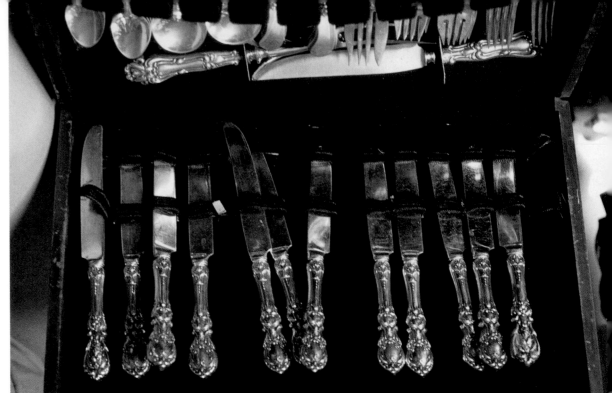

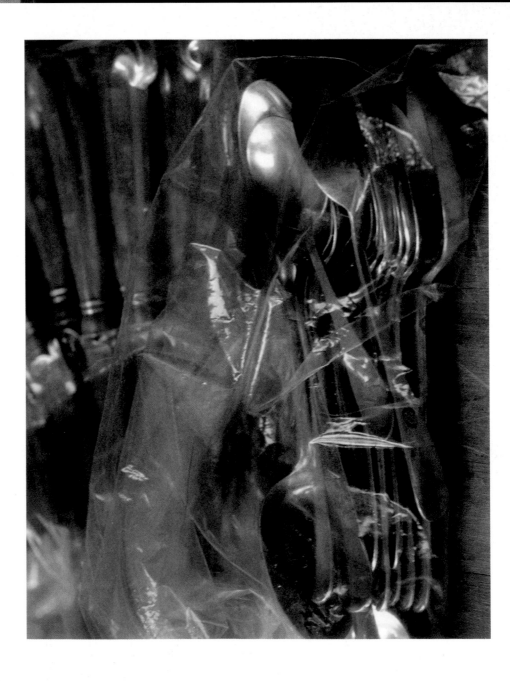

A variety of silver serving pieces add unusual character to a buffet or dining table, particularly on special occasions and holidays. Consider keeping them artfully displayed, in view and within reach, so they don't get forgotten. The more they're used the less they tarnish! Cradled in a silver epergne above are a trio of mismatched silver pieces—a carving knife, a large serving spoon, and a cake knife. Each is distinguished by a unique ornamental pattern on its handle. One was a house gift, the other two were picked up at different antique markets. When my husband and I were ready to cut our wedding cake in the wonderful old barn in which we were married in Connecticut, my mother presented us with one of her favorite old silver-handled cake knives, not unlike the one pictured here. She wanted us to have it as a keepsake of that special day. Since then it has been used over and over again to cut all manner of cakes and pies at many a festive gathering, but never another wedding cake. When the day comes to celebrate the weddings of our sons, I may stick it in my bag and hand it over at the crucial cake moment.

Opposite: Treasure the heirlooms that are passed down, but keep them and the memories alive by using them. The diminutive spoons at left were given to our sons at birth, engraved with their initials. I put them away for years and then one day, inexplicably, decided to polish them up and use them as sugar spoons or whatever task required a miniature spooner. The silver chest at the far left belonged to my mother-in-law. Like most of us, she rarely used her silver, but when she was in her eighties she would sometimes ask to see it, and opening the lid, as if for the first time, she would smile appreciatively. Above is a less romantic but practical way to store silver, in ziploc bags!

PAT,
YOU + JIMMY GAVE
THIS PITCHER TO MARY
AND MR ONK XMAS
AND I WOULD LIKE YOU
TO HAVE IT,
BESIDES YOU NEED
SOME SILVER TO POLISH
Love
Royall

Build character into a new space—house or apartment—with heirloom treasures, whether passed-down or collected. A few years ago, my parents set up a cozy pied-a-terre for themselves in a fairly newish condominium, and within weeks aged it with the addition of an old mantelpiece, old family furnishings, and some heirloom (sort of!) silver. As a housewarming gift, my sister's husband, Royall, gave them a beautiful old silver-lidded pitcher, seen above and on the dining table at right. The silver candlesticks flanking it are contemporary, but not those on the sideboard behind it, which were another present, thus the pink bows! The wallpaper and border were compliments of the former owner, and my mother had every intention of replacing them—"It feels too new," she declared the first time she saw the room—but once the furniture, silver, and artwork were in place, she found it worked. Note how the old silver reflects the sunlight and adds character to a room that was built less than two decades ago.

Above left: Sometimes tarnish can add a faintly elegant look to a beautiful old pitcher, particularly once you have tired of polishing it! Old silver pitchers —shiny or not—can serve up ice-cold water or a bouquet of wooden tulips.

Above right: When giving gifts of silver refrain from taping notes on them. Royall's yellow post-it message ended with (and here's the rub!)—"besides you need some silver to polish." When a well-meaning child decided to do the job, and attempted to remove it, she was horrified to find tape was removing the old silver plate! (Moral: Never leave a note taped on an old silver pitcher unless you mean it to be a permanent inscription.) Needless to say, the pitcher is now pretty black with tarnish, and the post-it inscription remains. May we suggest a notecard tied on with a string, or even a faded piece of ribbon?

RUST REHAB

Try collecting odd pieces of old silver like these to mix in and back up the everyday supply. They are particularly useful during peak entertaining seasons when securing a fork and knife can be difficult. Although there are products that deoxidize metal surfaces and remove rust, cures for rusty blades like these are unlikely. Prevention is the best method to stave off rust. Whenever possible, wash your knives immediately. Don't leave them wet overnight. If any stains are produced by hard water, detergent, or any other cause, they can usually be removed by rubbing them with a non-abrasive metal cleaning paste or liquid. Dishwashers can do in your cutlery by producing rainbow-like stains. When this happens, try wiping them down with a little lemon juice!

FADING FAST

Old photos unframed or framed in leather, wood, birch bark, cardboard, old brass or tarnished silver, tucked into diaries and journals, glued into scrapbooks and worn family albums—it's important to save your memories, and those of your family, in any way you can. An old friend and campmate of my mother's recently gave her a weathered leather album filled with pictures of her days at camp. Each little sepia snapshot is gripped at the corner by old-fashioned, black-paper photo corners and is neatly captioned underneath. My mother cherishes this album as those summers at camp were incredibly special to her. She had been very popular, and in her last summer she was awarded the camp's top "Spirit of Okahawis"

prize. She had no snapshots of those days and, in fact, very few of ours. The fires that destroyed our home had also destroyed all those perishable memories. Which is why, I suppose, I love to collect old photographs, even of people I know nothing about. They are substitutes, in a way, for our family pictures that will never be recovered. For my parents' fiftieth anniversary I put together a scrapbook of many of those lost images borrowed from other family members and friends. The images are xeroxed copies of the originals, but they satisfy us as we take turns paging through the scrapbook alone or with each other and our children and grandchildren. They help us tell the story of those bygone days in our own way.

Opposite: I love how his hand rests in the mouth of the lion-like St. Bernard, and how her paw is on his knee, barely touching the face of her puppy, held ever so gently between his legs. It's an early black-and-white polaroid. When I found the photo all the edges had softened, the black and white had gone to beautiful sepia, and my father's face was already a blur. I recently stuck it in my scanner, enlarged it, and placed it in an old, chewed-up leather frame with a tiny gilt border.

Turn your library into a photo gallery like I did when our wall space became overburdened with paintings and such. Park a photo here and there on the edges of the shelves to lean against the books. Although I love the overall effect and have found that there is an efficiency to pushing a framed image between two books (it's locked in place instantly!), the system does offer potential challenges—in particular, when you are searching for an obscured title.

How often do you take the time to really page through the mountain of photo albums scattered here and there throughout your home? Why not rotate some of your favorites out of the album and into your life via flea-market frames, like those seen above, or scan them into a computer and print out copies to tack onto the fridge. If you don't have the technical resources or a helpful family member to preserve your family's images, consider a trip to a copy shop, and presto, you've got memories to share in less than an hour. Frame them, as I did above, in period frames and you also have a memorable gift. If you want to start a photography collection, pick a theme, such as couples, or pets, or airplanes, or families, or children. Display your photos grouped together in vintage frames or scrapbooks.

Above left: I never went to Howe Caverns, New York, but I found this slice-of-a-log souvenir frame. Bookended literally by a biography of Carson McCullers and the zebra-striped cover of *I Married Adventure* by Osa Johnson, it's set up to present several generations in five perfect little branched ovals. I have yet to install family pictures of my own, preferring for now the five already in place!

Above right: A real Carter family portrait taken in the living room of our home in the fifties. The portrait of my mother above the mantelpiece was destroyed in a fire, so this black-and-white photograph is all that remains of it. One of my sisters scanned the original print and gave copies to each of us so we can look back and remember life in proper clothes in a proper setting.

Opposite: How often have you picked up an old family picture and longed to know who the characters were, and when and where the picture was taken? Take the time to carefully record all this information on the back of your pictures for future generations. My father did just that with this picture (taken in Virginia at Westover Plantation in 1910; that's my grandfather at far left with his pals Percy and Augustine!).

Sometimes a desk is just a place to rest, surrounded by a world of things and people that you love. Although mine, seen above and at left, has served me well through six books, numerous journals, letter writing, work projects, children's homework, and tucking pictures into scrapbooks, it has a life of its own. The stories, the stuff, the pictures it holds have grown over its three decades of duty. Scattered among the bric-a-brac of old alarm clocks, dolls, a yellow poodle lamp, an Infant of Prague, odd mugs filled with pencils, scissors and sharpies, various art projects, bits of shells and rock, and miniature wildlife is an important collection of family photographs. A wooden letter holder on the wall in back holds an assortment of postcards, loose snapshots, many Polaroids, and tiny works of art.

Opposite: Find your own special space to hang or gather your family pictures—for me it's my desk. Hunt for assorted frames of different shapes, materials, and eras at flea markets or at one of my favorite sources—the drugstore or Wal-Mart or Target. The right frame can enhance the romance of the picture, like the primitive wood-carved frame that surrounds my favorite image of Isak Dinesen, which is the centerpiece of my hodgepodge desktop exhibition. Or the photograph of my favorite view of the Rappahannock River, seen above it, covered simply with a piece of glass held in place by two metal clamps.

Above: Never pass up a unique little frame; you'll always have the perfect picture to place in it! And don't forget to inscribe information on the back. As time passes, it is harder to pinpoint which summer's day it was that you caught that fleeting memory, like that of my father and son taking time out in shorts and sneakers and a silly cowboy hat.

If you're in the neighborhood of New York City's West 25th Street between Sixth and Seventh Avenues looking for a place to park, you'll see the sign for The Garage—which is just that Monday through Friday, but on the weekends it is transformed to two levels of parking for hundreds of antique dealers and their stuff. There's a dealer on the ground level who specializes in old frames. But watch your step down the narrow aisle cluttered with suitcases and boxes spilling out frames everywhere. It's the kind of place (and there are lots of them!) that offers up assorted one-of-a-kind frames, such as those seen at left showcasing family photographs and children's artwork. Choose a frame that matches the mood of the picture, like the birch-bark heart frame transforming a picture of country sweethearts into a photographic valentine, the blue-tinted cardboard frame around a photo-booth memory, or the picture of my mother in a little black frame that just didn't do it justice. See its storybook transformation on the next page!

Don't you wish you had known your mother when she was a little girl? There was that memorable scene in *Field of Dreams* when Kevin Costner's character realizes the young ballplayer he is talking to is his father. Old photographs can do the same thing—roll the footage of the times we missed. When I first showed this childhood picture of my mother to her, the movie began: She was three, sitting cross-legged, all in white, on an old stump in her grandmother's backyard. This story led to another, and soon I was with her, in my mind, exploring the little wooden shed pictured behind her. The image of one of my sons, to the right, was taken when he was the same age as my mother in her childhood portrait. One day, perhaps, his child—provoked by this image of his father at three—will ask the same questions I did, rolling the frames of his childhood movie.

Above left: This picture of my mother at three, presented in this wondrous little picture-frame environment, is for me a marriage made in heaven! For years the photo lived in a normal black frame, until I discovered this amazing miniature, carved wooden masterpiece. You or your child can re-create an environment-enhanced frame like this by taking a simple frame and with a glue gun affixing miniature pine cones, little animals, or toys around it.

Above right: Wedged in between some of my favorite photography books is a black-and-white photograph framed in one of those cheap plastic box frames popular at the time. The environment, my son's youth, and the faded color of the print make it compatible with the childhood image of my mother at left. It's almost as if they were taken at the same time and in the same place.

Opposite: My child-sized orange and green writing desk is topped with tiny treasures tarnished by time and a collection of family pictures displayed in a variety of frames. At the top is a portable red leather picture case of family bow-wows (don't forget your pets!). The tarnished silver frame below it, which holds a picture of my father and son bearing the engraving "TIDY PRIZE, 1927" was a prized find from a tag-sale table for a dollar. The center image of my father and his loving daughters is framed in a painted drugstore classic. To its right is the little girl, seen above, all grown up—a portrait of my mother. I put it in a brass frame, matted with a piece of corrugated cardboard dabbed with watercolor. At the base of the slightly out-of-place, exotically tacky lamp is a photo-booth treasure of my husband and his mother rimmed with hand-painted blue cardboard.

He is making love with his wife on the roof
That's all right
But fifty years...
The cattle wait around as long as they can
then go off, like grenades.
The neighbors get heated over breakfast,
but they won't come down,
there's no legal loophole.
If a man want to spend as much time as that
on the roof of his house with his wife
That's all right by the law,
there's nothing improper in that.
Sometimes they noticed the grass beneath them,
and the woods around that, change
in their colors — the summer's
thin strokes, the slow flood of fall blood —
and the townspeople that lay down and died like ticks,
but they didn't care.
That was fifty years well spent,
he said, she said, as both
at last came down,
to the gold of garbage,
to the piano an oak again
to the television a camera,
the dog a frog
and the huge children they had forgotten about
waiting around minutely, in baskets,
to be born again.

Michael Dennis Browne

Years ago, for their 50th anniversary, I made a litle card-board scrapbook for my parents filled with photos of all of us taken throughout the years. The photograph on the cover, seen at left, of the two of them flanked by my brothers and a sister was taken in a field at Muskettoe Pointe. On the inside cover I copied a poem I read to them for many years on their anniversary. It was written by Michael Dennis Browne and celebrates the love of a couple who go up on a roof, leaving children, animals, and daily life behind, to make love for sixteen years. Each year I would insert the number of years they had been married. The last time it was sixty-three!

Today many families have digital scrapbooks or web-sites to share with their friends and family. I sill prefer the old-fashioned, hand-held album that can be passed around, or set on a table for anyone to browse.

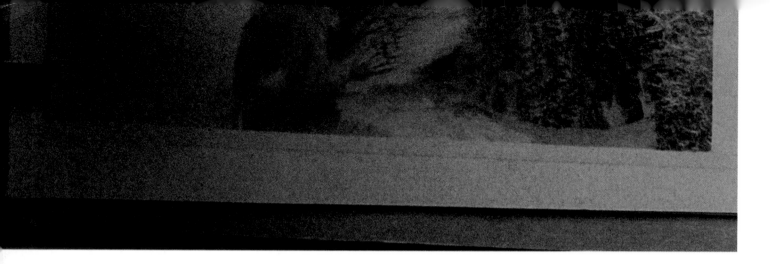

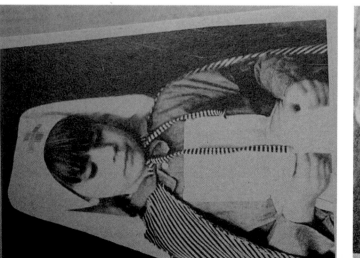

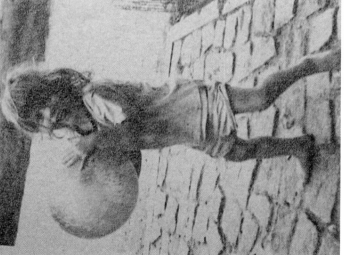

There are many ways to create a scrapbook or memory journal to commemorate those special moments in the lives of our family and friends—a wedding, an anniversary, a birth or birthday, a graduation. The pages you see sampled here from my parents' anniversary scrapbook were put together by laying out the pictures randomly (not in chronological order) and photocopying them on craft paper to give them a sort of low-tech patina. Today I would scan all the originals and print them out. I hole-punched the pages and the cardboard cover and tied them together with some suede strips. I recently borrowed the book to scan all its dog-eared pages to make sure it survives the next generation. Another way to recycle old family pictures is to create a family calendar decorating the months with time-sensitive pictures: Halloween costumes in October, photos of summer holidays in July and August, etc. Call out birthdays and anniversaries with photos from those events, and you do everyone a large favor! Check out software programs and do it yourself on your computer.

Above: Let's not forget about those furry or feathery members of our families—dogs and cats and birds for starters! Be sure to integrate them into your family scrapbook with images like the one captured here of one of the many Saint Bernards that competed with the number of children in our large family. A scrapbook devoted exclusively to the life of a pet is great to have and great to give.

Opposite, clockwise from top left: My youngest sister in her nurse costume; a hodge-podge of snaps in color and black and white juxtaposing different eras of family gatherings; a portrait of the artist (me!) as a young woman; my mother and father before they were married; another page of the family scrapbook—don't forget to note years, places, and names, which we did not!; an action shot that resembles the incredible reportage images from my favorite family album by Jacques-Henri Lartigue, *The Diary of a Century,* first published in 1970.

"A picture's worth a Thousand Words"

So if you are in the mood to save them — some things to consider...

Did you know that the famous proverb quoted above is, in fact, phony? Confucius never said it. It seems an advertising executive made it up to sell baking soda. Nonetheless, there is much to be said for what it implies — that an image can say a lot, sometimes more than words. But like the origin of this so called proverb, photographs need to be preserved.

There is an abundance of quality information on photographic preservation online. Go to Google or wherever you prefer to search, and type in "preserving old photographs" or the like, and you will come up with all the information you need, and more. In the meantime, below are my "Cliff Notes" of what I discovered.

⊘ Identify your pictures. It could mean so much to a future generation to know who they are looking at, where you were, and what the occasion was. It has been suggested that only photos that are thus labeled are worth preserving—I disagree. I have collected many an old photo with no clues given at all, except that something in the picture moved me to purchase it. Of course, I am also quite happy to make something up. Whether truth or fiction, inscribe your information with a soft 6B drawing pencil, available in art-supply shops.

⊘ Store pictures not on active duty in archival boxes or in photo albums. Serious collectors use acid-free folders and boxes, both of which are available online. If you choose to use a photo album, be sure to seek out acid-free papers and notebooks made of archival board. Clear plastic pages will work as long as they're made from polypropylene and not vinyl.

⊘ Beware of albums with magnetic pages. Conservators realized only recently that these types of pages had a very high acidic content, and photographs stored this way were deteriorating.

⊘ If you've been given or have found a wonderful old photo album, resist taking it apart. Albums were put together to tell a personal story, often with the creator's own handwriting, and shouldn't be tampered with. If, on the other hand, the snapshots have become loose, you can easily find paper corners to secure them again—no adhesives please! (The only exception is, of course, those horrid magnetic photo albums.)

⊘ Although I love the look of faded old photographs that show the patina of time, you must be careful not to let important photos fade or crumble. The best advice I ever read about storing your photos came from an online search on photo preservation. Go to about.com and search under Antiques, and in an article called "Preserving the Past," Pamela Wiggins suggests that you store your photos in the same kind of environment that makes you comfortable—not too hot, dry, cold, or damp. Temperature, humidity, and light are the three major culprits to avoid.

⊘ Although I've read that metal frames are preferable to wood, I have always preferred wooden frames. Unlike most plants, photos don't thrive in the sunlight, so find less sunny walls for display. When framing a photograph, it is wise to use a 100-percent rag matte board and remove wooden backing in old frames.

THE SECRET CUPBOARD

AN ATTIC CAN BE A SHOEBOX, A SHELF, A CUPBOARD, AS LONG AS IT HOLDS THINGS
WORTH KEEPING—OUR MEMORIES.

We all need a place to store our memories. As a child I discovered that place was called an attic. I was about six when I discovered my first—a dim, hidden world of boxes and trunks, suitcases and wardrobes tumbled on top of each other, filled (squished, even!) with old papers, letters, scrapbooks, school reports, clothes, lockets, and musical instruments, nestled next to paintings of forgotten people and places, mirrors, headboards, broken things, forgotten things, wondrous things, all sent into a benign exile by my two great-aunts. The door to this world was located in what was my second bedroom on the third floor of a stately brick house in Richmond, Virginia. I remember it was either very hot or very cold, always a little too dark, and always a little scary. My second attic, the one I remember most fondly, was again on the third floor of another old house in Richmond. Like most attics it was under the roofline, so you could stand up straight only in the center. There was a window toward the end of it, and that was where I set up my dollhouse and played out the stories of my imagination away from the clamor of my growing family. When I was thirteen we moved to the Northern Neck of Virginia, into a house on a river that had once been an old barn. There was no attic, so we played in the storage house. When we eventu-

ally moved to Muskettoe Pointe Farm, my parents turned a tiny attic into a child-sized playhouse for my younger siblings, but by then I was off to college and storing my memories in notebooks and journals and boxes that I could conceal in the back of a drawer or under my bed. When I left for New York City, all my treasures were stored in the top of the family barn. (I'm still searching for my Christmas card from Elvis Presley!) When I was expecting our first baby, we moved into the apartment we still live in today. Of course, there is no attic, not even a storage room in the basement. I needed to create my own little attic. And so I did—inside a tall, pine corner cupboard in our bedroom. When I open it I am greeted by a motley crew of dirty-faced dolls, teddy bears, and childhood toy pets worn down with lugging and loving. There are baby shoes next to storybooks missing their covers (I swear I can recite them from memory!) next to porcelain-faced beauties mingling with smurfs and booties and doll clothes, a red felt beanie covered with plastic Cracker Jack charms, and a Star Wars pillowcase. And sometimes at night I dream I can shrink myself down and slip into the cupboard and play like I used to amid all the clutter in those childhood attics that helped put me in touch with things worth keeping.

Opposite: Layers of memories—dolls, cloth cats, baby shirts, booties, and tiny bears-stacked up inside an old cupboard in our bedroom: our city attic.

We all need a place to store our memories. Get rid of the things that aren't worth saving and find a place, even if it's a few shelves in a cupboard, to store little things that stir memory and emotion. It's like having a three-dimensional scrapbook or your own grown-up dollhouse. Create the inventory from the relics of your childhood or your children's—a raggedy old bear, a doll, a favorite storybook, a tiny t-shirt or a pair of embroidered baby booties. Don't just throw them in, but arrange them thoughtfully, so when you take a peek inside all the memories will be lined up to greet you and make you smile.

Above: Attics seem to be a thing of the past; if you don't have enough room you rent a storage unit. That's fine for the sofa you're going to recover (some day) and the skis you may use again next winter, but what about those tiny mementos that will get lost in the bottom of a box, that are the treasures of your heart? Like my little folk-art cat, my old smudgy-faced doll, the miniature weathered sewing kit in her lap, and the first little dog of my childhood seen here. I say find a place for them a heartbeat away!

Opposite, top right: Arrange your artifacts like a tiny exhibit and you can share it with other family members like a 3D scrapbook. In the foreground, a plastic pink flamingo rests on a Star Wars pillowcase. A red felt beanie encrusted with plastic charms recalls the molasses taste and crunch of Cracker Jacks. *The Boy and the Drum* has lost its cover, but I still have the memories of reading it over and over to my two young sons. The little cloth cat leans against a tiny T-shirt identifying our first baby.

Opposite, far right: When you start to clear out your children's toys there will be some that tug at your heartstrings. It's okay to be a little sentimental and save a few of them like I have—a wind-up robot, an artistic smurf, a pair of baby booties. One day your grown-up children will thank you!

Opposite right: The door of the pine corner-cupboard that has been my hideaway attic for over three decades.

The Boy
with a Drum
David L. Harrison

CHIPPED BUT CHERISHED

It's only a matter of time before precious works of art created from plaster, clay, porcelain, and even concrete suffer the outward signs of everyday wear and tear. Witness the inventory of chipped things in my possession—angels, birds, elves, matadors, ladies, flamingoes, bowls, saints, dolls, and painted boxes! A chipped thing is very different from something tarnished. Tarnish, if found objectionable, can, in most cases, be easily removed. A chip is another obstacle altogether. There are chipped things that seem acceptable, like an outdoor ornamental statue in a garden, versus a chip on the lip of a teacup, which renders it unusable, at least for sipping tea. Chipping paint can sometimes be scraped off and repainted, but in that process the object may lose what seemed most desirable—a wonderful patina. When plaster or concrete chips, it is within the realm of possibility, particularly if you are at all artistic, to make a repair. But, like the proud matador, seen at left, who has lost his nose and much of his forehead and hair to accidents outside of the ring, chipped objects oftentimes have character and endurance.

Opposite: This little matador stands about 11 ½ inches tall, made of a plaster with a bluish cast that matches the faded blue of his bolero and toreador pants. The once golden embroidery that decorates his red capote and runs the length of his sleeve has been dulled by time, sunlight, and dust, but he still remains elegant like Manolete, the legendary Spanish bullfighter of whom he reminds me.

Garden ornaments—birdbaths, flamingoes, gnomes, and elves, the usual suspects—are ripe for the revenge of Mother Nature. Long after their flowering friends have drooped their heads and are carted off to the compost heap, they stand alone to be buffeted by winter winds and swirling snow and whatever nature can hurl at them from season to season. Not surprising then that their aging process is much accelerated. Last Christmas the funky birdbath, seen above, complete with a visiting (and very chipped!) red painted cardinal, was won by my mother in our family's "Nasty Christmas" tradition. For the last seven years on Christmas night, the adults of the family (that's everyone except the grandchildren, even though quite a few of them have long since qualified) gather after dinner for what we refer to as "Nasty Christmas." We each

contribute a unique gift disguised in wrapping paper, bags, boxes, or anything to deceive the audience regarding the true contents within, and draw a number to see who goes first. Number one chooses the first gift, but number two not only chooses the second but also has the opportunity to exchange the gift for number one's if it's more to his or her liking! That is, of course, when things get nasty! If a gift is well loved, it can pass from one person to the next until the final number is picked. The birdbath was nastily exchanged many times before it was ultimately won by my mother. That night we placed it in the garden outside the kitchen door (seen in another season, at right) where it has remained, in the shade of a towering ivy-covered mulberry tree, ever since.

Above left and right: Birdbaths are essential for birdwatchers and garden lovers. The former know that one way to attract more birds to your yard is to supply a place for them to flutter and sputter in water that is not too deep. The gardener, accepting that, also loves the way they decorate their gardens like the centerpiece of an outdoor living room. Birdbaths are as commonplace as a wheelbarrow, and as personal as a woman's fragrance. Gardeners who delight in something different may embellish them with painted borders or choose a centerpiece, like the little weathered cardinal, to add a touch of whimsy.

Opposite: The cardinal happens to be the state bird of Virginia, another reason why this birdbath and its tenant seem very much at home planted under an ancient mulberry tree at Muskettoe Pointe Farm. To attract real birds to your bath, treat it like you would a swimming pool—keep it clean and refill often.

A suitable ornament for a shady gothic garden, a damsel in distress for sure, this beautiful young cement lady reclining on a chaise has had her looks deteriorate from too much exposure to the elements. Her fragile, pale complexion and yellow silk dress have slowly been chipped away, transforming her former beauty to an almost appalling condition.

Opposite: A garden shed is the perfect hideaway in which to cultivate your collection of un-utilitarian garden objects. My Garden Hutte, inspired by Lilla Hyttnas, the red cottage home of the Swedish artist Carl Larsson, is brimming with vintage garden tools, paintings, and the chipped bric-a-brac of my old gardener's heart. Hovering above a still life of irises rests a legless pink flamingo—a garden ornament more suited for a front yard in Miami Beach than a farmhouse in upstate New York. Nonetheless, he and his mate, snared on a junking expedition, were quite a bargain, marked "as is" due to the missing limbs and the

paint-chipped visage. The delicate pink and gold-leafed teacup, seen in the lower right corner, has a hidden chip in the lip, but it did not when I bought it in Paris for more francs than I care to remember. Chipped cups are hard to drink out of but easy to admire as romantic decoration.

Above left: Gardens thrive on ornamental statuary—the crustier the better— accenting blooming things throughout the seasons. She appears to have been salvaged from the ocean's floor 10,000 leagues below, a broken coral beauty more at home among a garden of seaweed than the weeds of my country garden.

Above right: A stone guardian positioned at a gate or front door offers a decorative welcome. If you haven't found the perfectly chipped and weathered version, a good compromise is a new statue picked up from those ubiquitous statuary markets. To add a mossy touch, brush on a generous layer of buttermilk, cover with a plastic trash bag, and let it bake in the sun. The little stone fox with a broken nose, above, guards the front gate of Muskettoe Pointe Farm. No one seems to remember where he came from, but tucked under the branches of an ancient yew tree with a bed of ivy at his feet, it's safe to say he's here to stay.

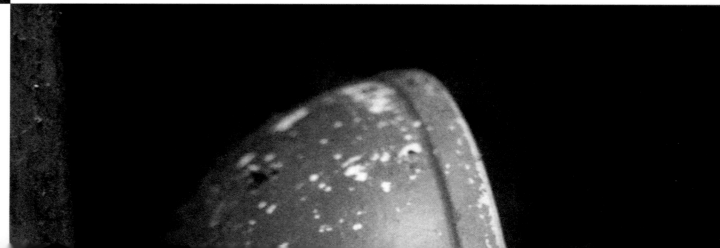

Above: One chip seems out of place, but when the object is chipped all over it's like a beautiful vintage pattern. A hand-painted bowl, encrusted with wildflowers of thickly dabbed pigment, rests on top of an old, painted cupboard. I can imagine it in a painting by Carl Larsson on a table in his garden at Lilla Hyttnas filled with freshly picked strawberries. Bowls chipped like this are off-limits for serving food, including, yes, freshly picked strawberries. Restrict their use to decorative purposes or as a subject to be painted.

Opposite, top left: A little old garden gnome with a gray beard is growing whiter bit by bit as time chips away the decades of paint to reveal the plaster beneath. His little gnarled fingers are twisted in place, not by arthritis but from years of holding a little gnome-sized wheelbarrow that is missing.

Opposite, far left: This damsel in distress, a weathered princess, rests quietly under a painting of giant sunflowers hanging among the clutter of collected flora and fauna. When all the color has finally

faded from her cheeks and dress, I might consider a touch-up with some acrylic paints.

Opposite left: The extremities seem to chip first, like the plaster tip of this happy blue elf's nose. A cross between a Smurf and the scarecrow in *The Wizard of Oz*, the elf has a head almost as large as mine. (To rescue a recent work such as this, take an artist's fine brush and dab on some blue and red paint.)

What do you call a gathering of angels? There's a gaggle of geese, a pride of lions, a clowder of cats, and a murder of crows. Is it a legion perhaps? In any case, a little worse for wear is this quintet of Thumbelina-sized painted wooden angels. Their musical instruments suggest they are a band. (Ah, that's it, a "band" of angels, of course!) Perhaps too many tours did them in? What is it about angels? They seem more popular than ever. Everybody's favorite has to be Clarence, that charming angel from Frank Capra's *It's a Wonderful Life*, who after 200 years finally snags his wings for saving George Bailey (Jimmy Stewart) from suicide. Whether a band of angels or a clowder of ceramic cats—chipped or not—display them together, there's strength in numbers.

Opposite: The former owner of this angel took the liberty of brightening up her original concrete gray tunic and eyes into a vivid blue, highlighting her dull locks the color of corn, and turning her mighty wings to a golden luster! By now her paint job needs a refresher, but I prefer her shabby chic. The painting behind her is a knock-off of a Matisse.

Mighty seraphim (each under five inches tall!) shine with a holy luminosity provided by silvery paint. The one with her hand raised seems right out of the Nativity story, greeting the unsuspecting Mary with a "Hark!" and then the staggering news that she will be the mother of God. The praying angel on the left has chipped extremities.

Opposite: Many find it comforting to live among images of Jesus, Mary, and the saints, along with religious medals and rosary beads. I am no different as I was raised a Roman Catholic. One of my favorite things is the embellishment of religous objects, such as gilding, the ancient art of applying a thin layer of real or imitation gold to many different kinds of surfaces. These life-sized praying hands, the centerpiece of my spiritual collection, give off a gold-en glow when the sun shines on them.

Random chips confirm their golden aspect is attributable to a layer of gild-ing, not the real thing!

Above left: Of all the saints, St. Francis of Assisi is probably not only the most loved but the most recognizable. His coarse woolen tunic, worn during his day by only the poorest Umbrian peas-ants, tied around with a knotted rope, reflected his vow of poverty and is still worn today by the friars of the Franciscan order he founded back in the twelfth

century. In this little image of him, gilded like the hands at left, he holds the Christ child, who grasps a stalk of lilies. The chipped places reveal the white plaster beneath.

Above right: Another image of St. Francis, trailing bits of plaster flakes, stands on a rickety corner shelf in the light of an old window. A dove nestled in his hands and a duck at his feet symbolize his great love of all animals.

A chorus line of eight statues of the Infant of Prague decorates a mantel. Each one is dressed the same, but the most special ones have hand-sewn gowns and capes, such as the one on the far left. The original, believed to have miraculous powers, resides in the Church of Our Lady of Victory in the Czech Republic. My collection of almost forty of such statues started about ten years ago when I picked up one with a glued-on head. I felt like I had rescued it, and since then have found more and more. They are all greatly distressed—chipped, broken, missing fingers and noses. I created a kind of spiritual rehab center for them. The idea was to try and mend them, but as time has passed I have decided I like them just as they are!

To my dearest wife Amelie,
and my little son Jean

I dedicate this work of art, which is a humble carver's
attempt to capture the love between a mother and her child.
You, Amelie, are to me the most beautiful Madonna, and
when you hold our son in
your arms your beauty is transformed a hundredfold.

With all my love,

Jean Jacques

Carved on the back of this rather large
16 ¼ x 19 ½ carved wooden portrait of a
mother and baby entitled "La mere et
L'enfant," signed by the artist J. Gagne,
which I found at a local flea market, is
the above inscription.

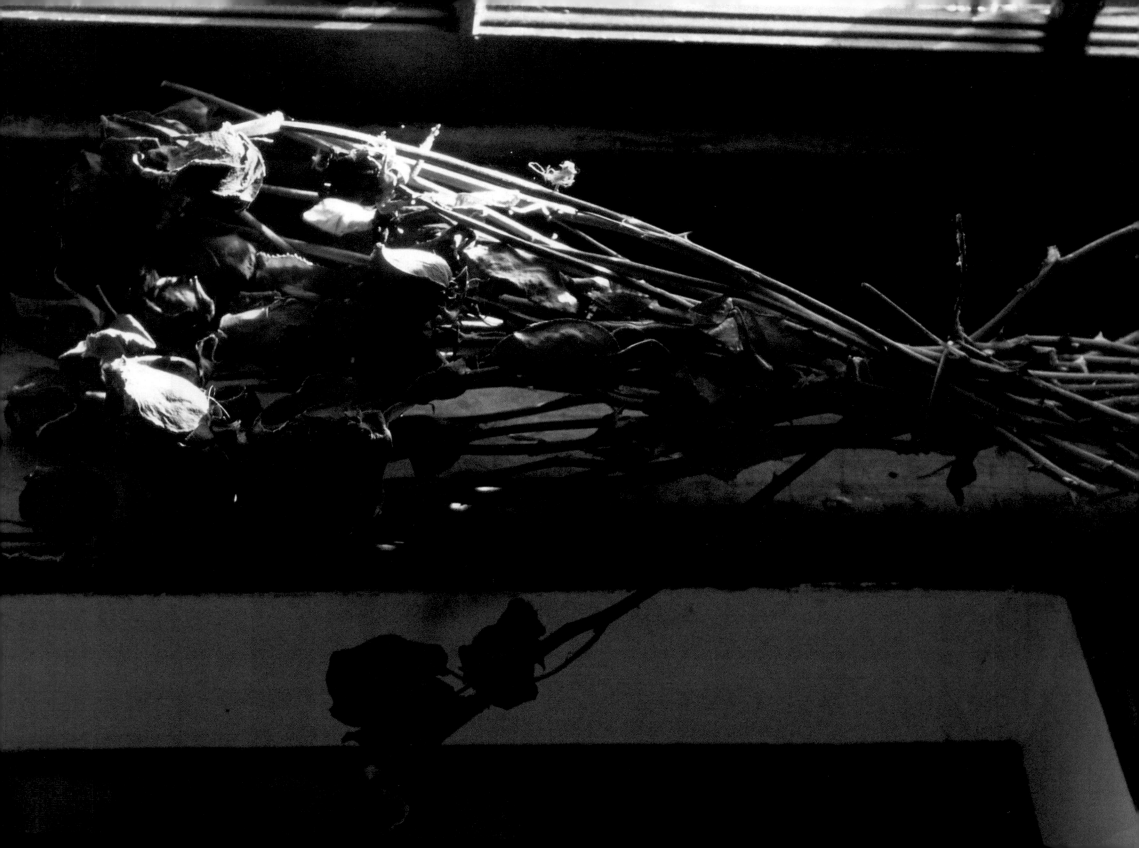

DRIED AND TRUE

What is it that provokes us to press old corsages into a book of poetry, or hang our wedding bouquet or roses from a beau in an anonymous corner of a room until their color has all but faded away and their scent has turned dry and dusty? Why do we pick the last sunflower of the summer and poke it in a corner of a makeshift potting shed? What is it about withered and faded flowers, or puckered strings of cranberries, hung over a fireplace from a Christmas ten years before? They stir up old memories, of course, and add to a room or a table or a desk a touch of mystery and romance and grace. Sometimes it only takes a little sentimental motivation to save that special blossom or bouquet. Sometimes the forgotten vase of flowers, instead of wilting, dries perfectly irrespective of your lack of attention. If, on the other hand, you are not of this temperament and too impatient to await those happy accidents, there are certain drying methods and particular posies (coming up in the following pages) that can immediately accomplish what I forever leave to fate.

Opposite: The bouquet of dried long stemmed red roses, seen at left, has been hanging from a nail in the corner of the kitchen for as long as I can remember. There was no ceremony when it was hung there, at least I can't remember one. The roses were more than likely a gift to one of my sisters from a "beau," as my mother would put it.

A friend arrived for dinner one night bearing the most beautiful bouquet of red roses. When I looked closely I discerned this unusual pattern, almost a dark stripe running through them. They were grown in Ecuador, and their variety is called "Intuition." I eventually cut off the stalks and placed them to dry in a petal-shaped dish on our porch. It took no time, and a summer later they are still with us, dried and true!

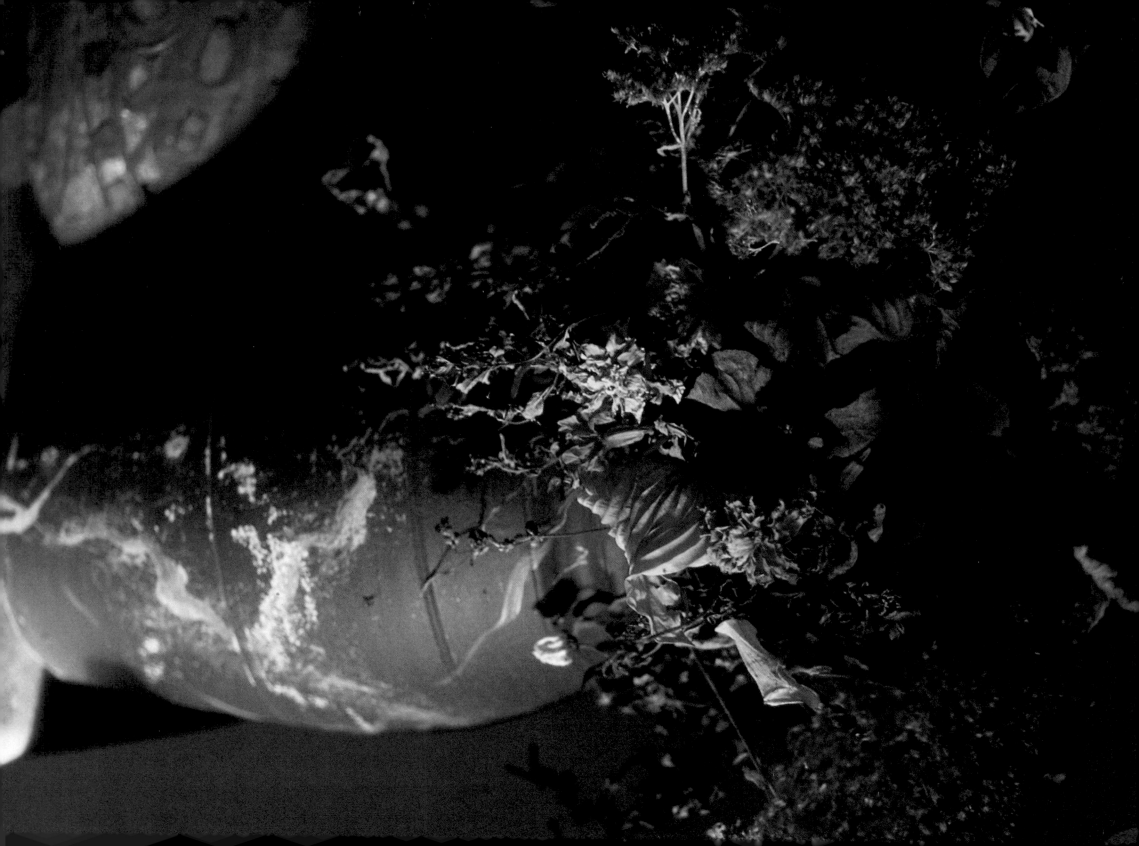

I love a home filled with fresh-cut flowers and pots of plants and leafy trees. To be greeted by them in city apartments, far from the natural resources of a country home, is particularly pleasing. But when those opportunities are denied or they fall at the bottom of your list of priorities, then let's hear it for replicas of those blooming things, either the artist's vision or the real thing, just a little withered!

Opposite: Although I used to try to keep a few plants blooming in our apartment, I found that because of weekends away, general travel, and a little forgetfulness these attempts more than often failed. Today I find myself relying more and more on low-maintenance solutions, like this everlasting bouquet of dried herbs and flowers. There are some very good artificial alternatives, as well, from little pots of lavender to long-stemmed paper poppies. Only the most discerning gardener could ever tell!

Above left: When flowers or even dried leaves are not an option, consider filling in with bouquets and scenes of nature from the artist's brush. A paper-covered tray, illustrating a red-headed child gathering autumn foliage in her dress, is a fine example. Floral arrangements were the primary subject of many of the Impressionists. Pick a bouquet by Matisse or Bonnard at a museum poster shop or online gallery.

Above right: Every autumn when the leaves turn their colors to red and orange and yellow, slightly desperate to prolong their beauty, I cut off long branches of them and place them in vases throughout our house in the country. Just like the trees outside, they slowly dry and curl and eventually fall, and I find myself raking up leaves not only from the ground outside but on the floor inside! (To dry leaves, just place cut branches into water and wait.)

Before you diligently rake those fallen leaves, like those scattered so delicately around a tiny white sculpture that reminds me of Georgia O'Keeffe, sweep some up to display in a more contained fashion inside your home. Think of a nest of them in a little wooden bowl or platter as a centerpiece for a Thanksgiving feast or use them as a bed for Halloween baggies of trick-or-treat candy.

Think twice before you throw out those dried-out wreaths or topiaries. The slightly pathetic wreath, seen at left, wired to an old weathered door was originally hung one Christmas as a form to embellish with holly, box bush, and magnolia. After the season was over and the dried-out greenery discarded, the little bare wreath was not. At Easter, someone stuck in some tulips, and in the summer some sprigs of lavender, and in fall a branch of yellow leaves, and then that second Christmas a string of wooden cranberries were entwined, and nothing else. Many years have passed since then. The cranberries are losing their color. The little wreath is part of the door now, no longer celebrating holiday seasons, but the everyday comings and goings of family. As the seasons change, extend the life of and create a history for your holiday wreaths or dried-out topiaries by adding to them your own personal accents or mementos.

Above left: I discovered this lichen globe (about the size of a large softball) at an antique shop and assumed it was some sort of handmade whimsy. I rested it in the top of a pottery pitcher, thinking it then resembled a dried topiary. Beside it lie the fuzzy dried centers of a couple of sunflowers, a pinky-brown dried-out hydrangea, and some old wooden knitting needles.

Above right: When a friend of mine was discarding some drying miniature topiaries, I scooped up this one. Somehow it didn't matter to me that their leaves had lost their color. Surrounded by pink flamingos and colorful floral prints and paintings, the topiary shape stands out like rusty sculpture.

Flowers, dried or artificial—tucked into a handcrafted wooden birdhouse, a collection of swirly painted clay pots, or adorning straw garden baskets or hats—not only bring the outdoors in, but are a charming alternative to the more expected flowers-in-vase motif. The natural shrine that has grown inside our farmhouse takes this concept a bit further. It started when I migrated the little lichen-covered birdhouse from a tree to the top of an old beaten-up wooden cupboard. Surrounded by paintings of cozy cottages and rural landscapes, it reminded me of one those rustic roadside altars stumbled upon on the back roads of Europe. I placed a plastic image of the Blessed Virgin on the perch next to the bird and one day the little pink dolly showed up, and a pair of papier-mâché rabbits, and eventually an unfortunate sour-faced girl with the body of a pineapple (hoping for a trans-forming miracle perhaps?). It reminds me of the crèche I set up each Christmas with Baby Jesus surrounded by his parents, shepherds, wise men, and all those barnyard animals.

Opposite, clockwise from top left: On a ledge, paintings of flowers on board and a funny straw hat mixed with bunches of the real thing; a close-up of three of my miniature clay pots, perfect receptacles for fragile dried branches; my birdhouse trio; an aged bouquet of Van Gogh's favorite flower; a gardener's hat rack filled with favorite straw brimmers; a straw basket with sunflowers past their prime and a postcard replica of a bird in paradise.

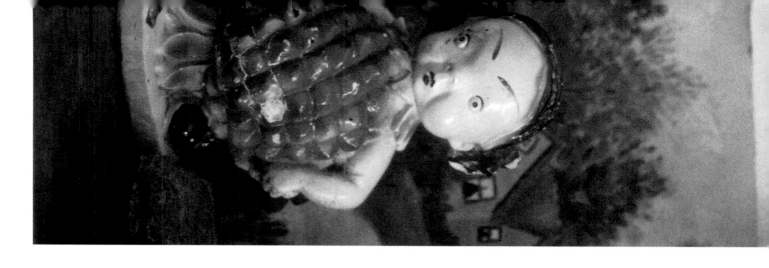

Recipies for Drying

My biggest dried triumphs have come from simply leaving well enough alone, just letting the flowers or herbs or leaves stand in their containers until the water has evaporated, and they eventually dry up naturally. If you would rather not leave it to chance, follow the suggestions below.

AIR DRYING

Air drying is the simplest way to dry herbs and leaves and flowers.

⊘ Strip away dead leaves.

⊘ Group stems into small bunches.

⊘ Tie stems with rubber bands or tie twists (see an example at left), or, if you're a purist, brown twine. Hang upside down in a cool, dry, and dark area such as an attic or closet or barn.

⊘ Allow them to dry for two to three weeks depending on the thickness of the stems or foliage. The fleshier the flowers are, the more drying time they will require.

DESICCANT DRYING

Some flowers wilt quickly and won't retain their natural shape or color through the air-drying process. Clean dry sand (believe it or not!) is the best agent for doing the job.

⊘ Fill a shallow cardboard box to the halfway mark with sand.

⊘ Lay the flowers gently on this sandy beach.

⊘ Sift more sand very gently over the flowers until all the petals are covered.

⊘ Secure box in a dry and warm area.

⊘ Flower drying will take from one to three weeks.

MODERN SAND DRYING

The only problem with natural sand is that it can sometimes be too heavy and cause damage to delicate flower petals. The modern substitute for sand is silica gel found at most garden centers, hardware, and craft stores. Although not cheap, you can use it repeatedly. Follow the same directions as for sand drying.

MICROWAVE DRYING

There is something about flowers in the microwave (kind of like tanning machines for humans) that just doesn't sit well with me, but be my guest . . .

⊘ Take one of your microwave-safe containers and line it with an inch of silica gel.

⊘ Lay the flowers on your high-tech beach.

⊘ Microwave on 50% power for 2-3 minutes.

⊘ You will see that the silica crystals will turn from bright blue to pinkish gray as the water is absorbed.

⊘ Remove flowers immediately and carefully.

⊘ You can remove the moisture from silica gel by rerunning the microwave on high for a couple of minutes.

⊘ Designate certain dishes for this drying process and don't use them for food preparation!

How often have you come home from a summer's walk with a clutch of wildflowers in hand, and, at a loss with what to do with them, tossed them in the trash bin? Do something more romantic! Secure them with what's at hand, such as package tie or twine, and hang them upside down to dry. Some will retain their color, like purple satice, but others, like my unidentified bouquet at left, will simply turn a generic brown. With that in mind, hang them against something with more enduring color, such as this faded and chipped blue-painted mantel.

Flowers

Perennials
Baby's Breath
Delphinium
Globe Thistle
Hydrangea
Roses
Money Plant
Straw Flowers

Annuals
Artemisia (Dusty Miller)
Statice
Sunflowers
Celosia
Larkspur

Herbs
Globe Amaranth
Lavander
Yarrow
Tansy
Chives
Sage
Lamb's Ear

Nothing's fail-proof, but the flowers above are good contenders for preservation. Each color and variety of flower dries differently. To preserve whatever color is left you should try to keep them out of the sun or eventually they will lose most of their natural pigment. Thankfully, the memories remain. At left is a close-up of a dried bouquet achieved through my lazy air-drying method of leaving well enough alone! So many flowers and herbs can be dried.

RUSTED

Most people look at rusty things as things neglected—not I! Well, yes it eats away at nice garden tools and chairs and gates and watering cans and keys and locks and hinges and bikes and toys and just about anything iron or steel that comes in contact with oxygen and water. You don't have to be a chemist to understand how much the three love each other, creating a process commonly known as corrosion. Rust is iron oxide, and truth be known, I love it. I think of it as a noble patina adding character to many things in and out of the garden.

No matter the season, we dine inside at a formerly rusty metal garden table discovered at a community yard sale one summer. Although I took steps to rid it of rust and refreshed the whole thing with sponged-on paint, the little specks keep seeping though like summer freckles on a little girl's nose. "Nothing's wrong with that," I say. But, not to offend seated guests, I camouflage the freckles with a series of favorite tablemats and vases of flowers and little saucers of votive candles and the like. And, although I wouldn't offer a friend a seat in an heirloom chair studded with rusty upholstery tacks, I might repurpose it (and have!) as an easel for a favorite piece of art.

A friend of mine once suggested that if I ever created my own fragrance it would be called "Rust," and there would be little rusty specks floating through it. I wonder how it would smell or sell? (Not such a silly suggestion from my friend, given how smitten I am with things bearing more than a trace of it.)

Join me in my Garden Hutte at Elm Glen Farm, and you will find an exhibition unlike any other. It is my Museum of Rusty Things—garden tools, furniture, architectural fragments, and mysterious bric-a-brac. Strewn about, they all share the common evidence of time and distress: rusty edges, spots, crust, and falling flakes.

Opposite: Speckled with rust, a trusty hoe—blade long since parted from its wooden handle—holds fast my flaking blue garden gate.

Above left: To let in more light and add architectural delight, I cut out a place for this old window, a scavenger find. Piled up in front is a free-form exhibition of rusty sap buckets—one holding garden markers that spell out in rusty letters "Mint" and "Herbs"—a knight in not-so-shining armor, a collection of veteran sickles, and, to the far right, a watering can painted green to ward off the taint of rust.

Above right: Old tin watering cans, rust and all, make charming garden decor or miniature planters. Here, a child's antique tin watering can is animated with storybook lithographs and streaks of rust from rivulets of water running down its sides, spilt by a little gardener's untrained hands. Today it wouldn't be a problem since now most watering cans are made of uninspired but rust-proof plastic.

Opposite: Made for each other, these trusted centurions—a weathered pale-blue shutter and rusted spading fork—guard the entranceway to the home of other dilapidated beauties. Good gardeners would shake their heads at the sight. Truthfully, this rusty reprobate was bought to serve a purely decorative function. The fork I actually employ is kept clean by wiping off the tines with an oily rug before storing. If rust appears, a wire brush should do the trick.

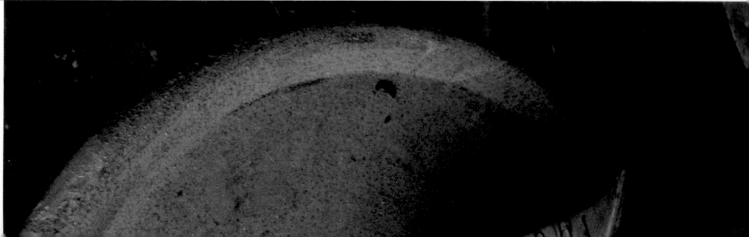

A garden and a *de rigueur* garden shed provide a fine excuse for collecting things that don't need to be weeded or watered. Add to that list surfaces that have acquired, by luck or benign neglect, a rusty patina. The garden is the special refuge of rust-touched pieces that may be ostracized in more formal environments. I certainly have a penchant for picking up derelict pieces with rusty pati-nas. Even my attempts to quell the rusty surfaces with paint seem to flop! An exception to the rule was a recent triumph—three rusted garden chairs totally transformed with one of those rustproof spray-on paints. I must admit I hated the result and left them out in the cold all winter hopeful they would regain some of their lost character. They did!

Above: Reminiscent of Monet's lilies, a green and yellow wooden frond floats on the surface of a little circular garden table, swirling with aqua water-colors and rusty ripples from untamed summer rains.

Opposite above: One might expect to see a magical caterpillar from *Alice in Wonderland* smoking his pipe on what appears to be a fantastic (albeit rusty) mushroom. It is truly an extraordinary garden whimsy created out of a cement foundation (possibly the base of a homemade birdbath?) and an umbrella-like metal top. Over the years it has acquired a rusty patina.

Opposite, far left: You can imagine the croak you might hear from this large garden frog seeking a better home than this rusty tabletop, a poor substitute for a succulent, green lily pad.

Opposite left: A rusty plant stand almost camouflaged among a crop of summer weeds and blooming stalks of catnip.

The fortuitous rescue of this once useful breadbox was not a minute too soon. Another few weeks left at the mercy of the outdoor elements—rain, snow, wind, and sun—would have totally removed not only the last vestiges of its lovely green paint but also the letters that spell out its original function.

Age Old Advice

If you are looking to add some age to a chair like mine, first consider just leaving it outside to let the elements affect it. You might consider scouring the leather with Brillo pads or the like.

To rust up tacks that appear too new or shiny, first scuff the surface with a piece of steel wool, then mix a concoction of iron sulfate and distilled water and apply it with a cotton ball. Iron sulfate can be found at specialty art suppliers.

Only neglect could have created the beauty of the blue chair that resides in my Junk Master's Atelier. (I don't know if chairs usually have genders, but this one is definitely feminine.) Actually, she is one of triplets, and although I don't usually play favorites, her markings (it must be said!) surpass those of her sisters. She came "as is"—distressed and rusted, unrecognizable I'm sure from her former self—rescued from a field attached to a desolate Victorian house, overflowing with the leftovers of a thousand once-distinguished homes. When I found her I gasped at the pain that she must have endured, and the humiliation. She was once a perfect Louis XIV chair, living in elegant splendor, I'm sure, until unknown circumstances changed her fortunes. I ransomed her and the other two for a couple of dollars each and carried them immediately to live in my Junk Master's Atelier. Her skin—once a fine leather upholstery—was ravaged and scarred by the elements. (I see it as a sign of character, like the look of a beaten-up old leather motorcycle jacket.) The upholstery tacks surrounding the outer periphery of the back and seat have turned to rusty jewels, which I prefer to the shiny ones they must have originally been. The old blue paint has slowly peeled away exposing the bare wood beneath. The other two chairs were missing seats. One I moved to the Garden Hutte to become an easel for a favorite old painting. The other lives near her sister in the atelier, her missing seat replaced with a perfect-sized metal tray. Transformed by age and hard times, my blue chair has no other function now than to please the eye of the beholder—mainly mine!

Plunk votive candles in miniature teacups to provide a soft light and touch of whimsy to a country dining table. These blue and white copies of a Delft pattern are rusty in spots, but never mind, the main culprit is melting candle wax that hardens in their bottoms. (To soften hardened wax, use a hair dryer.)

Above: It seems as though every old farmhouse had a bell to call the family to meals or to send a warning. Such a bell hangs under the stairway landing that leads to the loft of the barn at Muskettoe Pointe Farm. It is a handsome bell that has hung there for as long as any of us can remember. I have a feeling that the rusty patina was in place when it was first installed, and the salty air from the river has more than sustained it. Maybe it should have been hung closer to the house, for not once in forty years have I heard it rung.

Opposite, clockwise from top left: I call it my "Altoids" lamp, captioned as it is with the smashed Altoids tin affixed to the front of its rusty metal column. The pierced tin shade, made from a salvaged remnant, throws a beautiful light; although there are many authentic lanterns lit with real dripping candles throughout the interior of this old house, the one that hangs on a wooden peg outside the kitchen door is a repro- ducton lit with an electrified candle to withstand those blustery nights; an old wood stove highlighted with rusty spots

stands idle in a corner of our barn. One day I plan to hook it up, but in the meantime I look at it as utility sculpture; attached to the lower edge of these weathered shutters is a wrought- iron "shutter dog" with a curlicue tail to prevent it from banging when the wind blows; bunches of old, rusty keys that originally opened chests, doors, cupboards, and the like, but now are purely decorative.

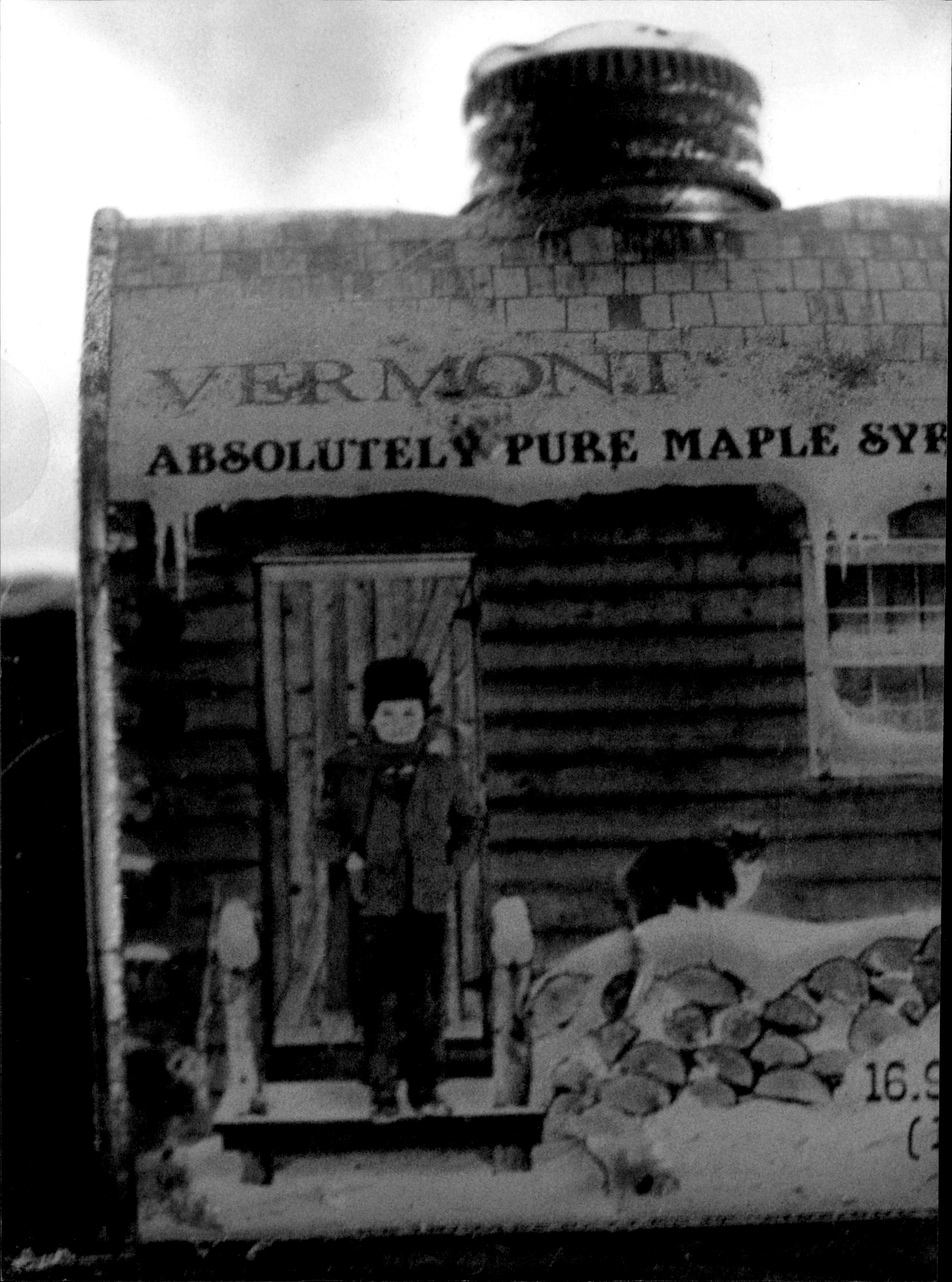
VERMONT
ABSOLUTELY PURE MAPLE SYR

No matter how hot it is, the snow refuses to melt or drip more than it already has from the roof of this tiny log cabin. The little boy on the stoop has never unwrapped the hand-knit scarf from his neck nor pulled the cozy cap from his head. The blanket of snow on the stack of logs has not moved an inch, nor has the contented cat. And until the rust that has attacked the cap of this four-inch high maple syrup tin destroys all the paint from this idyllic scene of a winter's day in Vermont, everything will remain just the same. It is a souvenir of someone's trip to the Brown Family Farm in Waterville, Vermont. The copyright on the bottom is dated 1984, although it seems so much older.

PEELING PAINT

Peeling paint reveals what's underneath—other layers of paint, colors, textures, and surfaces that describe what living for a long time can express: experience, pain, joy, memory, character. I have always preferred old paint on furniture and walls, front doors and shutters, even old paintings that are cracked and chipped and slightly faded. They remind me of the not-so-faint facial lines and wrinkles that record the millions of expressions I have made with my eyes and mouth. Paint can preserve old wood and pick it up with color. When I painted the yellowing wooden cabinets in our country kitchen I searched for an old greenish-blue paint I had seen peeling off the walls of an ancient fisherman's shack in the south of France. Futilely, I have brushed on layers of color, but I still have not realized the dream of those walls I covet. It is hard to re-create the character of old paint, which is why my favorite painted things were rescued from yard sales and flea markets and junk shops and even from the sidewalks of New York City. If the paint is chipped or peeling—even better! I have lived with paint peeling off of dressers, shutters, shelves, benches, baskets, desk, chairs, shelves, mantelpieces, mirrors, frames, tables, water pitchers, cupboards, and walls.

Right: A still life of simple things—a kettle, a knife, a bowl, a piece of cheese, a lemon laid out on a pink-and-white striped cotton cloth—cracked and pock-marked by too many years of sun and heat and the daily wear and tear of time. You cannot see its overly ornate gilt frame, which is in total contrast to the painting's humble subject. It hangs on the wall in our country bedroom; it is the first thing I see when I wake up in the morning and the last thing I see at night. I love to look at it closely and trace the map of cracks that lines its surface, like the face of the older woman I am becoming.

Above left: An aged and unframed landscape and a seatless chair exemplify the ways in which peeling paint can enhance the surfaces of different things that decorate our homes and lives. This watery blue landscape signed by E. E. Lombard rests easily on a substitute easel, what looks to be a Louis XIV chair with traces of old blue paint and no seat. They have cast their lot (and losses) together and provide an artful presence in my gallery.

Above right: An old work basket transformed into a flowery masterpiece has stood the test of time for more than thirty years in the front hall of my family's home. It brings to mind Monet's water lilies and inspires me to enhance and preserve similar old things with a paintbrush and a little imagination. Using an old dried-out basket as a canvas could be quite a challenge. Choose one that has a flatter weave, and keep your masterpiece simple. Keep in mind this work of art has been faded by years of sun. If that is the look you want (I hope so!) consider priming and sealing the porous surface with a tinted stain, and then choose a palette of soft acrylic paints. Place your finished masterpiece in a sunny place . . . and wait patiently!

Opposite: Just as antique buttons personalize an old cardigan, think of antique drawer pulls as charming accessories. I recently replaced a bunch of boring door knobs with a random collection of vintage ones, and what a difference! Here, a tiny bouquet blooms from a delicate knob on the lone drawer of a desk-in-distress, a yard-sale discovery. The owner explained he had started to refinish it, but found the old paint too stubborn and (luckily for me) gave up.

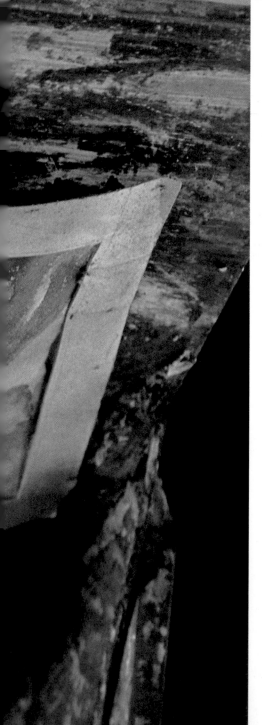

For the faint of heart who cannot abide the signs of distressed paint in their primary domicile, a garage or barn can provide the perfect hideaway. My Garden Hutte, a converted garage attached to a barn, housing all things that celebrate garden *joie de vivre*, is an anthem to my love of old paint. From the little Jackson Pollock-esque drop-front desk, seen at left, to the flaked and peeling chairs, tables, watering cans, pots, gardening tools—and, of course, garden-inspired paintings everywhere—it exemplifies the romance of paint gone astray.

Above: Take a putty knife to any old painted surface, and you can create the look of the artfully scraped-up surface on my beloved desk. The watercolors were found in a cardboard box (with about twenty others) hidden on a high shelf in a junk shop. They were done in the 1940s by the same artist, who signed them "R. Dvorak." To this day, I have yet to frame or hang them, preferring to keep them as footloose inspiration.

Opposite, top left: The full view of my little distressed desk surrounded by other

aged garden paraphernalia—a stack of hats, paintings, framed postcards, a Matisse poster, St. Theresa hidden behind drooping raffia—and its perfect partner, a pink and blue ladder-back chair leaving a trail of pastel paint chips whenever it's used! (The drawer knob, seen on the previous page, is hidden under the lowered writing apron.)

Opposite, far left: After years of banged-around duty, the pale-green tool box, seen on the top of the desk above, slowly reveals its true metal color. Hammers

and screwdrivers have been replaced by more useful tools of the artist—squishy tubes of paint and handed-down brushes.

Opposite left: To preserve some old memories, I rescued a couple of chewed-up postcards from mice who were dining on a Van Gogh landscape and Bloomsbury dishes, by tucking them (as is!) into a dime-store frame. On guard is a medieval lady-in-waiting with backup goldfish (by Matisse!).

The barn is an American icon, just like picket fences, dented pickup trucks, and apple pie. Way back when farmers sealed their barns with linseed oil, they sometimes threw in a little milk or lime, or blood from a recent slaughter. At least that's one theory about where the red came from. More than likely it sprang from a mixture of the linseed oil and a helping of rust or ferrous oxide, which was plentiful on farms and a poison to many molds and moss. What fed the tradition was the plain fact that red paint, even into the 1800s when it was produced with chemical pigments, was a bargain. For years I've promised myself (and my family) to repaint the weathered red exterior of our barn, seen at the lower right, which houses my Garden Hutte and a hayloft of collected junk. I am aware that new paint does serve a purpose in preserving old structures, but every year I fall more in love with its old faded color and can't bring myself to do it. If you share my dilemma, there is a solution—instead of repainting, seal the old paint with an exterior colorless sealant or choose a tinted stain. You can do this for many old painted surfaces that you love, like the faded green shutters seen above and at right, the little birdhouse below them, and all the peeling painted surfaces seen on these pages.

Above left and right: Old shutters are a dime a dozen—you can find them in almost any salvage emporium or flea market. They're often missing slats and are peeling layers of paint—just the way I like them! If they don't fit perfectly, you can cut them down or in half, as I did with the one pictured here. Every few years I sponge on some watered-down green paint to spiff them up a bit. The perfect camouflage is a tangle of leafy grapevines, as seen above.

Opposite right: Painted furniture should not be kept outdoors unless, of course, you covet the spotty effect exemplified by this do-it-yourself survivor.

Old painted furniture, such as this primitive green cupboard, the chair pictured at right, and the mantelpiece at left, has a penchant for showing its true colors—as time passes, the top coat wears away. Sometimes, the effect is most pleasing, in particular when the undercoat (in this case a mustardy yellow) complements the topcoat (a mossy green). As luck would have it, the undercoat also matches the floor, which had been painted almost the same color years before. The mantelpiece in the music room at

left used to be creamy white. I started to remove the old white paint, and after a layer or two struck black. I had the same experience with our living-room fireplace, so I decided rather than have two in mourning, I would leave some of the white. Not satisfied with the result, I dabbed on some green paint here and there. It seems to work with the lineup of artificial Chrismas trees above it and the lilies below. The unframed portrait of the pianist is suitable for this room dedicated to musical pursuits.

Left: As you can see, this mantelpiece no longer frames a fireplace, but an un-framed canvas of lilies. The cavity was covered when an oil furnace was installed, and the chimney served a different purpose. This is a perfect example of how you can use an old mantel to provide warmth to a room—fireplace or not!

Above right: When I first purchased "Heidi's chair" (that's what it reminds me of) it was losing huge flakes of black paint. After a good scrub with a wire brush, I removed most of it and in the process turned up some green. I can't take it down any further without applying some heavy-duty chemical stripper, so I live with it this way.

What gives great character to this simple hanging shelf, besides the collection of old pewter tankards and the tilty brass candlestick, are the helter-skelter brushstrokes of old indigo blue paint on the board behind them. Picking up on that blue are the circle of enamel numbers on my mother's beautiful old French wall clock ticking nearby. To replicate this chiaroscuro effect on a new shelf or wooden piece start with a white primer or gesso and, after it has dried, dip a variety of implements (e.g. a coarse brush or a sponge) into the paint and haphazardly smear.

If you are challenged by a cozy (tiny!) bedroom space, may I suggest hanging a shelf that's out of the way and can display a row of old botanicals cut carefully from a seed catalogue and framed in standard document frames that have been painted, as well as an abandoned bird's nest and assorted treasures. Not to cramp the narrow passageway between the bed and the wall, scrunch in a narrow bench that has been stripped of all peeling paint from years in the garden. It's just big enough to offer a stack of vintage cotton blankets at either end and a childish rendering of man's best friend in the middle.

The dresser seen at right, rescued from the front porch of a junk shop, was a bargain due to the fact that it was covered in flaking paint. (Life on a porch is not ideal!) When I got it home I scraped and sandpapered its surface as much as I could. Yet early on, every time a guest opened a drawer or walked past it on the way to the door to its left, paint sprinkles floated down to the floor. The tin frame on the mirror above doesn't have the same problem-luckily, it's a reproduction. The other furniture is all authentic, replete with falling sprinkles.

Opposite: To protect and camouflage the top of a peeling dresser lay down a pretty old piece of fabric and distract the eye with whimsical collectibles like a blue enamel drinking pitcher, a child's wicker doll bench, and a funny set of green pottery receptacles. The shade of the ladylike lamp has been camouflaged, too, with a pom-pommed valance from a set of old sheer curtains. The dried hydrangeas are replaced in spring and summer with live blooms from the garden.

The charm of old painted furniture lies in the way the pigments have turned during years of exposure to light and air and smoke, and the brush of cloth and hands and living, to an authentic dulled-down patina that is unique and, well, original! I would never touch the original paint of an old bench, like the green one seen above under the purple mountain landscape, or the yellow milk paint color on the drawered worktable under the windows. But, after scraping down to the older layers of black paint on the other two mantelpieces at Elm Glen Farm, I decided it was time to add new color to the remaining one in the dining room. The bright school bus yellow brightens things up, in particular during the darker days of winter. The old metal garden table in front of the fire has been repainted a few dozen times with a sponge and some watered-down latex paint. The hardest thing to cover is the candle wax that is continually dripping down and the rusty freckles that tend to appear when the humidity is high. The blue corner cupboard was white until I had that yen for color and sponged on some layers of blue. Would I paint the original wide board floors? Never! But if they were new floors or floors that had already been painted, then yes, as I already have in other rooms of the house.

Opposite, top left: This little reproduction of *The Angelus* by Millet hangs on a newly painted kitchen cupboard. I had seen some shutters on an ancient French house in *The World of Interiors* and tried, with at least five applications of green and blue and yellow paint, to match their colors. I failed, but I feel certain that in time all the cooking smoke and sunlight will create that longed-for patina.

Opposite, far left: The color of this hand-made box with leather hinges and a carved-out rooster (used for gathering keys, not eggs) was another inspiration for the color seen above.

Opposite left: The candelabra on our make-shift dining-room table, in keeping with my new passion for color, is burning crayola-colored candles.

There is nothing like the look of paint that has faded and cracked the old-fashioned way—slowly! The red and white paint on this pewlike bench is the real thing. It's probably not particularly comfortable because it's quite narrow, which is just as well as it's now home to a collection of thrift-shop landscapes, a unique red wooden squirrel, and a sewing tin. Underneath are stacks of books, mostly on gardening, hence the watering can. The shiny white paint on the kitchen floor is not original, but neither are the floors.

Indulge your collector's passion and allow it to take over a room of the house! It's a celebration of peeling paint in my Junk Master's Atelier, where you'll find peeling paintings, hundreds of them, collected for years from thrift shops and flea markets, as well as paint peeling off of furniture—the mantelpiece, chairs, and a pink chandelier.

Holey Paintings

My passion for collecting old paintings has sometimes clouded my senses (and good sense) about their condition. Small gashes, rips, or punctures like the one seen in the painting here, have never deterred me. Others might think they <u>are</u> the beauty of the artist's work – not ! ! I can live with them along with other signs of time's betrayal, such as faded colors, chips, snags, the frayed edges of the canvas. If the work of art speaks to me, I love it... warts and all ! If you are not of the same mind and would like to mend some tiny flaws, here are a few suggestions. But take heed to follow them only if we are talking about junk masters, not family heirlooms or masterpieces. These should be taken to a real art conservator.

FIRST AID FOR A TEAR

Gingerly place a band-aid of duct tape on the back of the canvas behind the rip. Alternately, apply a fine piece of linen or muslin over the back of the tear using a spot of white glue. If there are frayed edges in sight, tuck them away before surgery!

TO CLEAN SURFACES

Leave well enough alone, but if you must, barely dampen a soft cloth and try to lightly remove surface dust and grime. Dip the cloth into a diluted mixture of a mild detergent and warm water. Don't wet the canvas. You don't want the water to soak through and spot the back of it. Too much soap and water will dry out and crack the pigments. Don't use a household spray cleaner on an old painting.

THE "WONDER" WAY

Another way to "dry clean" an oil painting is to ball up fresh Wonder Bread slices into doughy little pellets. Rub one at a time gently over the surface of the painting. The dough balls crumble, so to prevent an even bigger mess, spread newspaper under the project. (Also good for cleaning old, fragile wallpaper.)

TOUCH-UPS FOR THE BRAZEN

If you're brave or bold with paints, touch up a missing spot on a painting with Magic Markers or crayons. For watercolors, try Caran d'Ache, Swiss-made crayons that, when dipped in water, give a watercolor effect.

ALL OF THIS IS AT YOUR OWN RISK!!!

They say you can't choose your family, but I beg to differ. Hanging throughout our house are family portraits my parents chose to adopt after ours were lost in a fire. If for any reason you have a yen for some ancestors to add a little dignity to your walls, be my guest! And while you're at it, there's no reason you can't hang a portrait, or a facsimile of one or two, of the founding fathers. Although I don't like to recall the fire that destroyed our home and our family's photographs, books, portraits,

and all those cherished things that seem irreplaceable, I am certain it taught each of the eleven of us in some way what's really important. We lost everything, including our beloved Saint Bernard, but our family survived. Within a year, my parents had found a new home for us just up the road from the one that we had lost. It was familiar territory, and in that old farmhouse set back from the shores of the river we all loved, we started over.

Above left: Meet Sarah, a new ancestor we named, with the sweetest smile but no frame and not much of a provenance, except that the artist was English, as were both sides of my parents' families. She hangs in the living room over a stately highboy cluttered with ancient leather-bound books, an old glass vase, a jar, a hand-blown bottle, a jade-green Chinese pot, a peach-colored pot, and a slightly out-of-place but authentic family photograph.

Above right: If you have a child who loves reading about the lives of American presidents and men and women celebrated in history, collect their portraits to hang on a wall as seen here. Besides Abraham Lincoln, there's Lord Nelson, George Washington, and Robert E. Lee. There is no evidence of paint peeling from their heroic visages because all except the wooden profile of Lincoln at top are printed reproductions. The only cracks are spied behind them in the old plaster wall.

Opposite: The venerable gentleman who presides over the mantelpiece in the dining room is a great-great-grandfather on my father's side. He's not actually, of course, nor are the others—they're stand-in ancestors, all of them. What's more authentic are the Christmas stockings hung below him. Many of the old hand-knit ones are in dire distress from years of candy canes poking holes in them. We line them with a new sock each year so Santa's booty remains secure, at least until Christmas morning!

A perfect example of how random old paintings can be gathered together in harmonious discord—framed and unframed, still lifes and portraits, cracked, torn, faded, perfect—is exhibited on a wall in our apartment. Over the three decades we have lived here, this wall in particular has subtly reflected the changes at large in the look of our city home. The old English bench, softened with homespun checked pillows, settled in this spot when we first moved in. Situated in the front hallway it's a perfect spot for parking bags, pulling off winter boots, and welcoming the dog. My favorite out of this hybrid collection of flea-market and antique-shop masterpieces is the largest one in the center, of a woman in the winner's circle surrounded by her animals. It almost looks as though the dog was an afterthought added later. It was in its present cracked condition when I bought it, looking as though it had possibly survived some sort of fire. The pie safe to its left, another original furnishing that has long been a storage space for spirits, was brightened up with a coat of green paint (and a potted wooden sunflower) a few years back.

WORN AND WEATHERED

Old wood warms the heart and home. Picture old wooden floorboards supporting wooden tables and chairs, cupboards, beds, and carved wooden objects—fish decoys, growling bears, birds, miniature canoes, shoes, doll furniture, and religious statues. Imagine stacks of firewood ready for burning in fireplaces decorated with old wooden mantelpieces. Contemplate a rest on an old bench made of old gnarled tree branches in the shade of an old pine tree near a stream covered by an old wooden footbridge. Walk across it and you might see old wooden birdhouses and feeders swinging from the branches of a towering oak welcoming woodpeckers, cardinals, blue jays, yellow-breasted finches, and brazen squirrels. Fences made of old pickets and split rails create the borders between one field and another. I think my bones must be made of old wood, my love for it is so ingrained.

Opposite: The entrance door is the first welcome one receives. With that in mind, choose carefully the message you send! This aged paneled door has surpassed its duty, having been pulled open and banged shut by every member of our family, plus so many friends, a thousand times over. Old doors like this are ubiquitous in salvage yards and on the internet.

Old wood paneling, floors, beams, and doors are often the trademarks of old houses. The paneling nailed to the walls and the architecture of old cupboards, like those seen at right, helped protect the walls from creeping dampness and insulated them from the chill or heat of the season. Wooden beams laid across ceilings or built into corners to strengthen the structure offered a cozy embellishment in contrast to the stark white walls of commonplace plaster. All of these character-building accoutrements are readily available, and when they are built into a room can warm it right up just like an open fire burning in a fireplace.

Above left: Beautiful old wooden cupboards and doors require complementary old hardware. If you can't find the real thing, a good reproduction will do. Most home-supply stores have a huge array, such as the original old cast-iron handle of the cupboard.

Above right: A pair of old keys dangles from a handmade nail hammered into old wooden beams that stand on either side of the dining room fireplace.

Millions of old keys are to be found in antique shops, flea markets, and on the internet, but the chances of your finding one to fit your old lock is pretty hopeless. Key collectors take heart in our forgetfulness; they prize a key more for its distinctive shape, size, and workmanship, not the lock it will open.

Opposite: The addition of doors is a good example of how to add instant heritage to a new kitchen. This interior wall is a hodgepodge of old wooden doors, with a row above them of primitive brown German pots once used for storing cheese. The pair of doors to the right opens onto a small hidden sink, a wooden counter, and various shelves for storing daily staples. The pair to its left provides room for stacks of ironstone plates and oversized serving dishes. Both storage spaces were once standalone corner cupboards.

Though they look as if they were carved from old wood, this baker's dozen of nesting eggs, gathered in a crockery bowl, are plaster! Originally tucked under unsuspecting hens to make them work harder, today they fool unsuspecting breakfast guests looking forward to a fresh omelette.

A Good Fire is a Safe Fire...

Have your chimney inspected by an authorized chimney sweep once a year. The buildup of nasty creosote can cause a chimney fire. A good inspector will also look for cracks in the base of your fireplace and will fill them in so live cinders don't travel under your house to a beam. The sweep will also climb up on the roof and check out the chimney from top to bottom.

Make sure your fireplace is protected by a screen, that the flue is open before you begin, and that all charming rugs and wooden stools are out of reach of a leaping spark. Keep a fire extinguisher handy.

Although I tend to leave the ashes in the fireplace all winter, when the time comes to remove them I have found an old galvanized trash can will hold them until they go out to the compost heap. Make sure your ashes are totally cooled off when you collect them.

It's autumn. The telltale signs abound—the skyline of brilliant leaves, fields of pumpkins and dried cornstalks, the slight chill in the air, and the curl of smoke rising from our chimney. I must confess it is my favorite time of the year, the season when I can perform my favorite ritual—gathering firewood. For me the kindling is the most important ingredient and it's gathered all year long from the grounds around our house. I always start my fires with a layer of crumbled newspaper, then dry kindling, and occasionally cheat with a fake starter log to get things going. I prefer to use those hardy, long wooden kitchen matches so that I am able to light the newspaper in several places using one match. When the kindling has caught I position a couple of skinny logs gingerly over it. When the logs begin to crackle, I sit back and enjoy!

(According to the *Old Farmers Almanac*, hardwoods such as oak, maple, cherry, or birch are the best to burn. Make sure the wood is cut in late winter or early spring so that the hot summer sun will dry and cure it—a drying and curing period of at least six months is necessary.)

Old wooden mantels that frame a fireplace, as seen at right, not only focus the fire but the whole room itself. Chairs and sofas are gathered around it, toasts are made in front of it, chilled hands and feet, and even frosty paws, are warmed by it. If a room is in want of character, add a mantel—with or without a fireplace. The mantel at right was once white but I decided to sand it down to the original paint, which, as you can see, was not an interesting green or mustard but an uninspiring black. However, my mother told me that many of the old houses in Virginia can be dated by mantels that were painted black to mourn the death of George Washington. I quickly decided this was the reason for the black paint, and resolved never to change it. The low wooden bench in front of it (possibly meant for kneeling?) is the perfect height for making a fire or sitting to get warm.

Above left and right: Our blackened mantelpiece is a wildlife refuge of sorts for carved wooden creatures such as this pair of Mutt & Jeff-sized bears. Overseeing the coming and going of the sturdy kitchen matches, this little fireman carved by J.A., we presume, is forever on guard!

Opposite: The room with the blazing fire is where everyone wants to gather on a cold winter's night. A fire can be faked many ways these days, from decorative electric logs to gas ones almost as cozy as the real thing. Old mantels are easily snagged in salvage yards all over. To resuscitate a dying fire I use the indispensable brass blow poker seen at left. (To order one, visit the Victorian Fireplace Shop at www.gascoals.net. Or try www.jeffersonbrass.com for similar models.)

Old-time treasures add texture and authenticity. They are the surprise ingredients that add personality to the way we live. Case in point, the little chest of twenty-seven drawers celebrated here, which I found myself drawn to when I spotted it in a cluttered little antiques shop. The old wood was appealing, but mostly it was the handmade-ness of the piece that I loved. Someone, a carpenter or craftsman or both, decided he or she needed a storage place for a random collection of nails and tools, and without much forethought—nor a blueprint, I would imagine—created this little multi-drawer wonder. The little drawers were designated to store the nails sampled on the exterior. No longer! I have chosen to use it to store tiny purposeless treasures, like minia-

ture steel dogs, an alarm clock, two baskets, and a pair of binoculars, as seen above. If you were to inspect the cargo of the diminutive drawers, such as the one on the lower far left, you would find the kind of little plastic charms and prizes that used to be the prize booty inside Cracker Jack boxes. One of my favorite non-plastic treasures is the tiny pair of wooden shoes dangling from the handle of one of the drawers, seen at the lower left, and the Thumbalina-sized, hand-painted dustpan balanced on the ledge of one of the larger drawers seen at the top far left. If one day I clean up my act and live in a more monastic space, this is one of the souvenirs of my old cluttered life that would have to follow me there.

Think of things carved of wood as you would a string of pearls or diamond earrings. They are the warm jewels of your home, adding their texture and fine lines to larger pieces of furniture—old or new. Over the years I have collected a range of wooden objects, most of them fairly primitive, to bring a touch of whimsy or grace to the top of a bookshelf, a desk, a dresser top or bedside table. My favorite is the carved mother embracing her two sons seen on the opposite page at the top right. It reminds me of me and my boys clinging to each other for dear life. I keep it next to my bed and love to pick it up and feel the grain of the wood and its weight—it was once just a chunk of wood from a tree in Jamaica.

Above: Though it recalls the nursery rhyme, "There was an old woman who lived in a shoe," this carved wooden shoe is home to only a candle nub. Beware of wooden candlestick holders like this; if the candle burns down too far you may have more light than you bargained for!

Opposite, clockwise from top left: A pair of hand-carved and painted love birds perched on a branch; my favorite carving of a mother and two boys signed by the artist, a wood carver from Jamaica; a century-old slenderly carved image of the Blessed Virgin; handmade doll furniture—a tiny table and chairs set for tea with a miniature painted tea set made from walnuts; a stringless violin, stripped down to its bare wood, for ambience, not music.

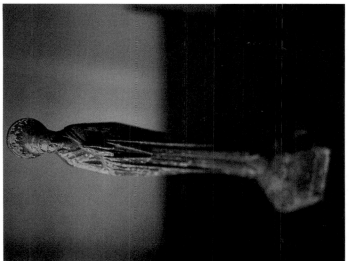

Trap stakes are the tall pine trees to which the fishermen attach their nets in the waters that lap the shores of the Tidewater area of Virginia. Eventually, they turn to driftwood and pile up on the shore. My mother gets credit for finding new life for them in many purposeful creations; one being the trap stake partition seen at left. Not too long after we moved into our apartment, I was stumped for a way to divide our very long living room without impeding the flow of light from the windows at the back. The solution was a set of five trap stakes secured tightly between the floor and ceiling with another one running perpendicular across them at the top. Once in place, I embellished them with a primitive watermelon sign in the center, a straw guitar above it, wooden fish decoys, and, swagged across the top, a beautiful old American flag edged with a yellowed cotton fringe. If you are similarly challenged, lumber and salvage yards can supply you with trap stake alternatives. And for those who, like I, had to give up beautiful old casement windows for more modern replacements, look carefully at the windows in our living room and you may detect the black masking tape mullions I adhered to the plain squares of glass to give them instant character!

143

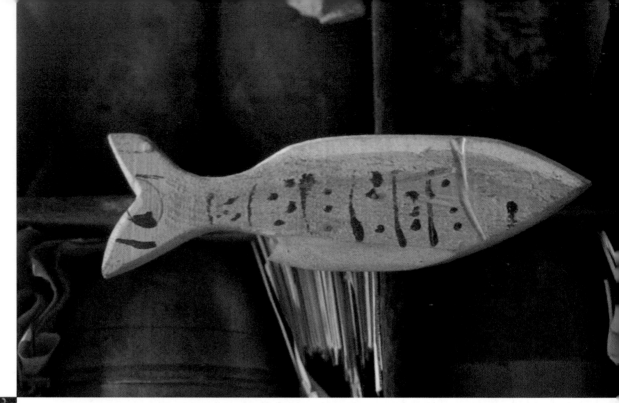

The headboard seen above, cobbled together out of a pair of trap stakes and an old floorboard, was a happy solution to the futile search for an old bed that would fit a queen-size mattress. After the headboard was secured, a metal bed frame with a box spring and mattress was pushed up against it. To add height—a higher bed is so much more old-fashioned and allows for more storage underneath—place a set of those ingenious plastic bed risers under each caster (available at places such as Bed, Bath & Beyond or online at www.comforthouse.com). Above it hangs a remnant of an old chenille bedspread stretched across an old wooden frame. From the posts dangle signs of wildlife—fish and bears, and Mardi Gras beads. Perched on the headboard ledge are three little miniature houses, and on the far right, above layers of old fabric pillows and Beacon blankets, is an image of my mother and father in a carved wooden frame.

Opposite, top left: Save your children's memories. The little wooden cupboard filled with miniature storybooks and other childhood souvenirs gives my grown-up sons (and me!) great pleasure. The photograph of Babar was taken years ago at a Thanksgiving Day Parade. The little red and white ruffled pillow, below it, delivered lost teeth to the tooth fairy.

They still love to wind up the music box on the lower shelf and watch Pierrot, the little French clown, sway to a nostalgic tune.

Opposite left: Looking for the perfect catchall for miniature treasures, photographs, or stray papers? Check out the wooden boxes turned into handy storage units on the wall, near a mirrored dresser bedecked with beads and necklaces. Before cardboard took its place, wooden boxes with dividers were used for shipping. You'll find them for sale in lots of country shops or flea markets. Just turn them on their sides and secure them to your wall, and then embellish with a whimsical trophy like a hand-carved and painted yellow fish!

Old wooden birdhouses, or replicas crafted out of weathered wood and painted in fanciful, often distressed, milk paint colors, became the darling *objet* of country collectors a few years back. Very often the birds lost out since the collectors started stationing them on porches and sunrooms as folk art décor like those seen above. An even cleverer idea is to take a picture of a friend's house and have some crafty birdhouse builder re-create it. It's the ultimate housewarming present—and one that will never be returned.

Above: The top of an old country cupboard nailed to a wall under a covered porch is home to stray pots and bowls, and a trio of birdhouses. Before investing in something new to provide a home for garden paraphernalia, search for an old cupboard with ready-made patina. If you choose it as a home for a birdhouse collection, don't count on too many feathered tenants showing up. Birds like their nesting homes at least five to ten feet up in air and certainly out of the way of predators. If you are serious about providing a home for birds, do a little research or be disappointed. Birds are very choosy about where they nest. Aren't you?

Opposite top: A high-rise replica of Muskettoe Pointe Farm stationed in the riverfront gardens by one of the builders who helped restore the original house so long ago.

I love what happens to wooden things left outdoors. The rain, the wind, the frost, and the snow soften their hard edges and colors. Left to live in the wild they become romantic, like the flora and fauna that surround them. The wooden flower boxes I found abandoned on the sidewalk in New York and dragged to the country are poetic when filled with a cargo of pink geraniums. My wooden songbirds, birdhouses, and flower girls planted among my herbs and wildflowers bring such delight.

Opposite, clockwise from top left: A quartet of weathered wooden gartifacts (my made-up term for garden artifacts!): a painted silhouette of a girl in a gardening hat— R. Springer, perhaps?; an unusual breed of cardinal, striped in faded colors and nailed into a little stand; a duo of lively colored songbirds perched out-side another kitchen window; a cozy birdhouse that has seen many a feathery tenant come and go.

Above: Looks can be deceiving! The worn and weathered window box, with a clutch of violets blooming out of it, fell apart a few years ago, but I was able to salvage it by tacking the old wooden front piece onto a newer plastic one.

Ancient mulberry trees, like the paper mulberry trunk shown at right, are no relation to the true mulberry tree. They show their age with the most outrageous gnarled whorls and bumps and exaggerated formations, suggesting the trees of romantic English novels, slightly scary but beautiful and unusual, like plumper versions of Giacometti sculptures or arthritic hands. They have inspired me to love outdoor benches, fences, trellises, and sculptures fashioned from imperfect tree trunks and branches, which fit so naturally into the landscape they feel as though they might have sprouted from an errant seed or root.

Above: A pair of slightly decrepit benches crafted from random branches and twigs have a decidedly Adirondack spirit, although they rest under a pine tree hundreds of miles south of that region. I fear the day is not far off when they will be reduced to kindling!

Opposite, far right: The split-rail fences that meander through the fields have withstood many seasons of outdoor weathering. When they reach the silvery maturity of the one seen here, it's only a matter of time before they break and fall and must be replaced. I stockpile new ones out of doors so that they can get a head start on the weathered look I love.

Opposite, right: A North Carolinian egret made of driftwood reaches for a tasty treat of New York honeysuckle.

Hidden in a tangle of overgrowth, this little shingled hideaway brings to mind the story of *The Secret Garden*. It has been a refuge for children's play, a writer's words, a gardener's toil, a place a little out of the fray where time passes not with the clock but with the shadows of the day. If you are so inclined, seek out an old shed like this one, or build one of old wood and shingles, and escape to it with your book and candle.

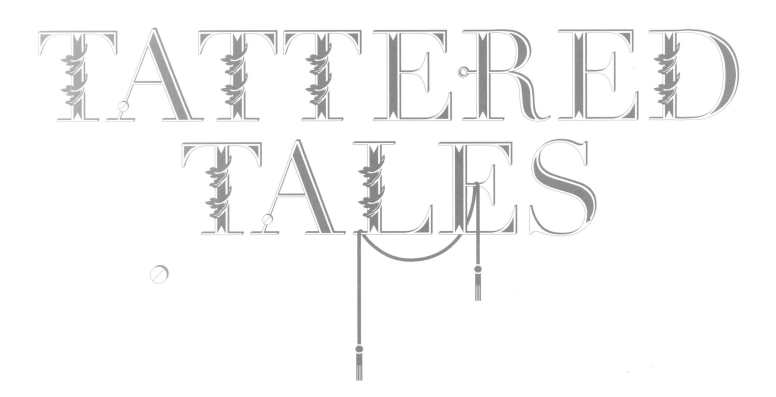

TATTERED TALES

So many of the friendless young heroines in literature were comforted in great libraries filled with volumes of old books. The greatest of all was of course Charlotte Bronte's *Jane Eyre*, which was published in 1847. On the very first page Jane has been exiled from the drawing room by the heartless Reed family to a small breakfast room, happily supplied with a bookcase. She picks out a volume— "one stored with pictures" (Bewick's *History of British Birds*)— and climbs into a cozy window seat, where she sits "cross-legged, like a Turk," and draws "the red moreen curtains nearly close...." She was "then happy," fearing "nothing but interruption...." That's what old books, bookcases, and libraries offer all of us—an escape and some happiness.

I have always lived with old books. The ones I remember most vividly lined the walls of the living room at the river-side barn my parents converted for year-round living when I was twelve. There were the blue and gold volumes of *My Bookhouse*, a series filled with classic children's stories, fairy tales, and nursery rhymes. There was *Little Lord Fauntleroy*, *The Secret Garden*, *The Wind in the Willows*, *Elsie Dinsmore*, and the *Five Little Peppers and How They Grew*. Many of the books

I had not read, but I recognized them by their dust jackets or the decorations that embellished the spines facing out from the shelves. *Lorna Doone* was a bluish green, and *Green Mansions* was bright yellow. Like Jane Eyre I would find a cozy spot and page through them looking for pictures. The night our house burned down, and with it all those books, was the night I began my search to replace them. I have found them in secondhand shops tucked away in the most remote places, in book stalls in London's antique markets, on flea-market tables, even abandoned in boxes thrown out with the garbage on the streets of New York.

My books are old friends that keep me company, stacked up next to my bed, tilting in precarious piles in the living room, sagging in built-in bookcases, or nesting in baskets here and there. Sometimes I am drawn to a book simply by its cover (I have five copies of the famous zebra-striped *I Married Adventure!*), or sometimes because it is a book that I cannot live without, such as *Kristin Lavransdatter*. Although I own some first editions and have started to accumulate early editions of the Modern Library, I don't think of myself as a serious book collector, just an old book lover.

Opposite: Three tattered classics held in place by an old bronze bookend—a replica of a bridled horse—atop an old desk in my family's cozy library.

Books warm up a room, giving it character and substance. The floor-to-ceiling bookshelves at Muskettoe Pointe, seen at right, are no exception. This is the coziest retreat in the house due to the warmth of hundreds of old books bound in fine old leather, cloth, and paper, whose sheen and the gold of their titles is reflected as the sun touches them through the facing windows. The old pine ladder is to aid a search of the upper shelves. Consider collecting series of books such as the novels of Thackeray or C.P. Snow, or books on history. As long as you're not fussy about perfect condition, you don't have to pay a fortune. In our shelves in New York City I have matching sets of O. Henry, Robert Louis Stevenson, William Faulkner, and Ernest Hemingway.

Above left: The standing globe in the family library is probably older than most of the books in the shelves. Its view of the world is hand painted on old paper that was attached to a big wooden sphere and cradled in a fine mahogany stand. Globes make a nice accessory to a library. The problem with old globes, like old maps, is that although they are beautiful, they are not always very helpful as they quickly become outdated.

Above right: A friend of mine collects old Bibles, many of them in rather poor condition; however, their beauty lies not only in the word of God illuminating their interior pages, but in their formidable size and the strength of their handsome bindings, some of them leather. She prefers to keep them handy, not just on Sundays, but every day, stacked up on little side tables next to good light and comfortable chairs.

Opposite: A library can be an entire room dedicated to books or just a shelf of books in the living room. Book collectors would not approve of the way the sun shines on the bookshelves in this library—the result is faded covers. Nor would they approve of too many books squeezed together on a shelf so that the top edges are worn away when we pull them out. Books are a responsibility, but books locked away in a dark room and never seen seem such a waste. Love your books and display them in a place where they can be enjoyed.

Bedrooms and books go together. I would wager that more reading gets done in the bedroom than any other room in the home. And even though you may have a comfortable chair or chaise, as we do in our bedroom, seen above, most reading probably occurs in bed before the lights go out. Books (old and new or a mix) warm up a room whether stacked on a bedside table, perched in a little hanging shelf, or flung in a chair.

Above: When the original old rusty casement windows were replaced in our city apartment bedroom, I hid the ugly new ones with three pairs of old green shutters. I have often considered adding a floor-to-ceiling bookcase, but that would mean giving up walls dedicated to favorite paintings. So, instead, there are little pockets and piles of books everywhere—in a blue basket on the floor next to the bed, in a little hanging shelf on the wall above it, on the seat of a refurbished thrift-shop armchair, and on the painted wicker table next to an old chaise longue, a favorite spot for reading.

Opposite above: My favorite boots rarely go into the closet: I like to look at them, and they're there when I need them! That's also the way I feel about my favorite books—I like to have them around, like this stack piled up on a wooden footstool hidden behind the boots. The little memory box on top is a sort of shrine to the Virgin Mary.

Opposite below: Though I believe in keeping books in sight and within reach, some, such as diaries and journals or precious little books in fragile condition, may do better stowed away. This slightly chipped European enamel breadbox makes a fine refuge and a bright display.

Miniature books are defined in this country as no more than 3 inches in height, width and thickness. Some are smaller than a penny! Thought of as a novelty today, when they were first printed (the earliest is attributed to about 770 AD!) they were designed to be carried and concealed by the reader. Due to their size, these tiny tomes deserve to be displayed separately from their larger kin, and lined up side-by-side they make an even more distinctive statement. I lined mine up—tiny to tall—on a little hanging shelf. The only one that really qualifies as an official miniature is the first little volume at right, a leather edition of *Macbeth* measuring a little over 3". The tallest is a paperback of *The Member of the Wedding*, signed by Carson McCullers, and those in between are *Wee Willie Winkie*, *Our Village*, a dictionary, and two little marbleized volumes extolling the virtues of prayer. They reside with a gallery of other tiny treasures.

As many books are piled up on the floor and on tables, benches, and stools in our living room as are stored in the bookshelves at the other end. Is this any way to treat a book? No, but for many of us who can't get enough, eventually there is nowhere else to put them. I pile them up as gently as possible in places that won't cause accidents, such as under a table or at the end of a sofa as a resting place for a lamp, both seen above. Carl Sandburg's home, Connemara, (open to the public) in Flat Rock, North Carolina, should give all of us book lovers faith that there is always room for a book that you love. On a visit there some years back, I was happily astonished to see books everywhere, even in the dining room and climbing the edge of the stairs.

Above: "Let sleeping dogs lie," like this one—Charley, our black Lab, spread out on a sofa softened (and protected from black dog hair!) by layers of vintage spreads, blankets, and pillows. The blue painted table is home to piles of old and new books, and shelters mountains of them below. Above the sofa is a large embroidered reproduction of *Washington Crossing the Delaware*, after the painting by Emanuel Leutze. It is flanked by a pair of three-dimensional carnival plaques and another pair of weird thrift-shop paintings.

Opposite above: Choose a special category of books to collect, such as this stack of doggy tales. Visiting children plunk themselves down in this pint-sized, ladder-back chair and help themselves!

Opposite below: Beautiful little books are like small bowls of flowers that never wilt! I had no intention of ever reading this slim French volume, *Histoire d'un merle blanc* by Alfred De Musset. I bought it for the beautiful Art Nouveau cover. It is only six inches high, cost a dollar, and romances everything near.

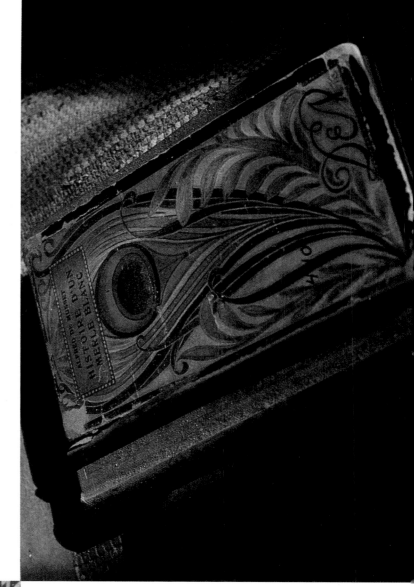

HISTOIRE D'UN
MERLE BLANC
ALFRED DE MUSSET

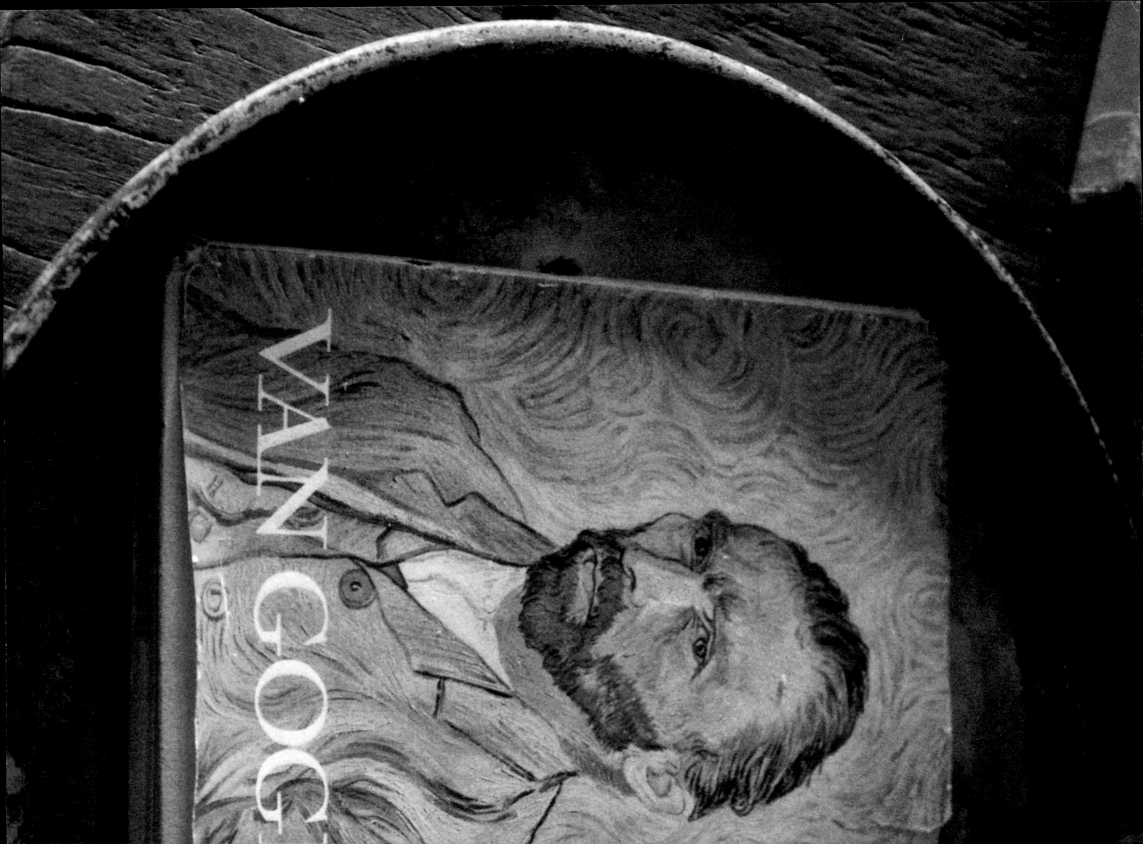

I think of all my books as works of art and display them with the same reverence (well, sort of!) as if they were originals. Our apartment is filled with Van Goghs, including self-portraits—unfortunately, they're only reproductions, such as the one on the cover of this little art book that's served up on an old tin tray with a trio of Chinese matchboxes. I like the way all the blues swirl together and don't even mind the tattered edges of the book's jacket.

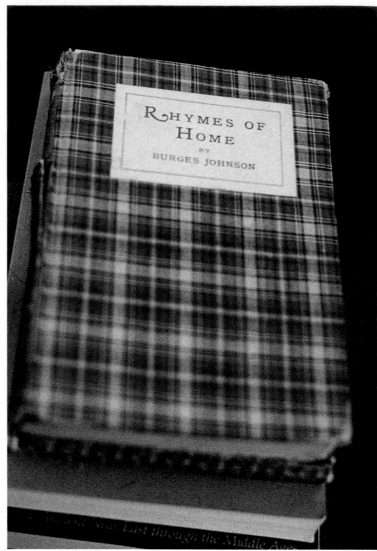

Book collectors all eventually share the universal challenge—too many books, too little storage space! When we moved a baby grand piano into the front parlor of our house in the country, it not only gave the room more focus (music, of course), but also provided a new surfaces for displaying books, books, and more books. In addition, it set the tone for specific themes of art and literature—Matisse on the music stand and Colette nearby.

Above left: The top of our piano has become a salon for artists and writers such as Colette, pictured on the cover of one of my favorite paper volumes, *Pages choisies,* found at a secondhand book store.

Above right: An exception to the likes of Colette is a plaid cloth-covered edition of *Rhymes of Home* by Burges Johnson, published by the Knickerbocker Press in 1910. Fabric-covered books are hard to find and often pricey, unless, of course, you are willing to live with those that have not endured the years so well—this one is splitting along the spine.

Opposite: I am sure a true pianist would disapprove of the way I have covered every inch of our baby grand with books and Beaux Arts bric-a-brac. Propped on the music stand, along with an album of sonatinas, is a thrift-shop copy of Matisse's *White Plumes (Les plumes blanches)* and another painting underneath. Art books, mostly on the Impressionists, are layered on the top along with other artful finds—a red toe-shoe sculpture, an alabaster apple, a plaster compote of fruit, and a stringless violin.

Most of us associate gilded edges with Bibles and prayer books, but although some of the earliest gilded pages, from about 1450, were on religious works, the art was applied to a range of books. Gilding served a very functional purpose, preventing dust from falling into the pages. According to Salisbury Bookbinders, a revered bookbinder in Carmarthenshire, Wales, gilded edges today can also protect a book from the effects of atmospheric pollution. The prized volumes of my red book collection, seen on the table at left, were discovered in a Paris flea market. I love the craftsmanship of the red and gold embossed covers and the way they glow like a sunset on the water.

Opposite above: Every Christmas season I bring out an old feather Christmas tree in place of the chipped red vase that is the centerpiece of the old ship card table. One year, to make things festive, I surrounded the tree with piles of red books that now remain all year long. There's something nice about displaying books together that are the same color, size, or subject matter.

Opposite below: One of the cardinal rules for protecting your books is to store them out of reach of sunlight. But all of my bookshelves are in view of windows, which is why these beautiful old gilded volumes shine so. (I shall make a resolution to remember to pull the curtains or shutters before leaving the house!) The first seven volumes are a series called *The Boy Travellers*, published in 1886. I boldly admit they were bought only to be seen, not read, as well as the three others—a farmer's report from 1901 (I liked the gilded sheaves of wheat at the bottom of the spine), a French edition of Tolstoy's *Infancy and Adolescence*, published in 1886 (it sometimes sits with my red collection), and who could resist a book called *Snagged and Sunk*? (I loved the charming image of the moose!)

ADDRESS UNKNOWN — by Kressmann ...

BY THE WATERS OF MANHATTAN ☆ ☆ ☆ Reznikoff   BONI

PAINTING AS A PASTIME · WINSTON S. CHURCHILL

Moon Face — Jack London

A DOG ON BARKHAM STREET   M. S. Stolz   HARPER

Marguerite Steen

How to treat a Book

As much as I love my old books, I regret that I have not cared for them as well as I could have and should have. In other words, don't do as I have done — except when it comes to collecting as many as you can, including any book that you love, no matter its condition nor how many copies you already have.

I am, I admit, a different kind of book collector. Though I appreciate those who are more disciplined and principled, it's possible no one loves old books more than I! I have some first editions, and books with original jackets, and even signed copies, but what makes old books valuable to me is more ambiguous. I cannot resist a book with character, even if time and misuse have caused it distress like the slightly shabby crew seen at left. If you are more responsible than I, check out *Book Collecting 2000: A Comprehensive Guide*, by Allen and Patricia Ahearn, or see the tips below for preventing this from happening to your books.

⊘ Don't build bookshelves next to windows. The light leads to paper decay and causes spines to fade and rot. But if you do, at least pull the curtains or close the shutters when you're not around.

⊘ The ideal temperature for books is between 60-70 degrees Fahrenheit. (Sounds pretty good for book owners, too!) You might try a humidifier for the dryness and a dehumidifier for the dampness. My books in the country suffer from too much coolness and dampness, which can make them moldy. In the city they suffer from dryness caused by overheated radiators, which can crack old leather and make paper brittle. In my barn, which has no electricity and is a real no-no for book storage (as are basements and attics), I hang little bags of sand, which you can make yourself or pick up at the hardware store. When they become fully hydrated, you can dry them out in the oven or under the hot sun.

⊘ The larvae of certain beetles, silverfish, and cockroaches feasts on the starches and glues found in the spines of books. Look out for those little piles of brown dust! And, bewarned, mice would love to make a nest out of the choicest pages of your favorite books of poetry.

⊘ The experts at Salisbury Bookbinders are very opposed to sagging bookshelves. (Yikes, don't look at mine!) They cleverly suggest using a block of wood to prop them up when this occurs. They also suggest you avoid placing shelves against an outside wall that may be damp, or at least leave a good inch gap between them and the wall, and do keep them away from radiators (I am in trouble!). Oh, and to keep your books ventilated, don't push them all the way back to the wall or smush them together.

⊘ Beware of bookends with metal inserts that go under books and may abrade the bindings.

⊘ Store very large books flat, but do not place others on top (ouch!) as they may damage the spines.

⊘ When removing a book from the shelf don't hold it by the top of the spine or pinch the spine with your fingers; either way you might damage the binding. Instead push the books on either side of your selection toward the back of the shelf and pull the book out holding its sides properly.

⊘ Do not mark your place in a book by setting down a pair of glasses (I've done that!), by turning down page corners (yep!), or by leaving the book face down or up (once or twice!). Never use rubber bands to hold a book together (I thought I was so smart!). Instead tie a wide strip of cotton cloth around the book (I like the way that looks, too). Do not use paperclips, staples, and pins, unless you like those rusty, untreatable, indelible marks!

⊘ Romantics take care: Do not press flowers in books as this stains the paper—unless, of course, you're totally obsessed, like me, and really couldn't care less!

Collecting sets of books not only fills a bookshelf quickly, but adds a sense of harmony and authenticity to your library. The ubiquitous set of encyclopedias that filled the shelves of every family in the fifties has now been replaced by online research, but that hasn't stopped me from displaying my old Britannicas. Pick a favorite author—Ernest Hemingway to Robert Louis Stevenson—and you're bound to find a matching set in leather or cloth. The Modern Library has been reproducing matching volumes of literary classics since 1917. Today, there are 750 titles, from *Jude* to *Sister Carrie*. Go to www.modernlib.com for a little history on how the Modern Library started, and for advice on how to start or add to your collection.

Above left: This ultimate reader's armchair is covered in a blanket-check wool. An ottoman upholstered in faux leopard skin offers rest to weary feet and a copy of Carl Sandburg's *Honey and Salt.*

Above right: Why are some books more valuable than others? This volume of poetry, *Honey and Salt* by Carl Sandburg, published in 1963, is a first edition that I paid only twenty dollars for several years ago. Normally, the original dust jacket would add even more value to its status as a first edition, but being all tattered and with a faded spine to boot dismissed this advantage. I must admit what attracted me to it was the romantic portrait of Sandburg with that dashing scarf wrapped loosely around his neck.

Opposite: The substantial bookshelf and its twin, seen above, fit snugly against the back wall of the living room. The blue and gold twelve-volume series to their left—*My Bookhouse*—is identical to the one I pored over as a child. The orange *Child Craft* series was a later discovery. My sets, which were bought almost twenty years ago, cost less than forty dollars each. The photograph of the chair framed in gold echoes the gilded book edges. The patchwork cushion lining the sagging seat of the old hickory Adirondack-style rocker beside it affords some comfort.

Paperback books, although incredibly friendly, portable, and good in bed—they don't break your nose if they sleepily slip from your hands—are on the bottom rung when it comes to collectibility. They're considered dispensable, no matter their age. One exception, for me, are the striking orange English paperbacks published by Penguin. I started picking them up quite accidentally while studying English literature my junior year in London. They cost around three shillings and sixpence then. Not long ago, an article in *World of Interiors* illustrating the flat of a cool young artist who had filled a floor-to-ceiling bookcase with hundreds of Penguin paperbacks reignited my passion. I became obsessed with hunting them down, in particular those from the 1960s and earlier. I have only just begun, as shown by the paltry collection stored in a hanging blue shelf, seen at left, in our country bedroom.

Above left: Don't do as I do and stack books on top of each other—you'll crush their spines. And don't expose them to direct sunlight—you'll fade the covers and weaken the bindings. Or do as I do, and enjoy your books any way you can!

Above right: An image of a camellia by Consuelo Kanaga, framed in a plastic box, has found a home among other venerable artworks in one of our bookshelves. The gilded pages shining beneath are from a prayer book and diary.

Opposite: A sewing box, a piece of pottery, a grape plate, and a faceless painting are stand-ins until more orange Penguin paperback are scavenged to fill out my hanging blue shelf. The orange binding is tremendously helpful when scanning the endless shelves of dusty volumes in second-hand bookshops.

Very often it's fun to collect books by theme—books about dogs or children's readers. Or, possibly the silliest reason of all—by color. Sometimes I fall for a book just because of its dust jacket, as in the set of Zane Greys seen at right, or because of a charming illustration like *Honey Bunch*—a cover without a book, seen above. I love displaying all my red books together, especially at Christmas. Motivations can overlap, for example red books about dogs, seen in the little pile above.

Above left: I don't remember if I found this cover of *Honey Bunch: Her first Summer on an Island* completely detached, or if it was dangling by a thread from the rest of the book. No matter, I love the charming illustration and display it in front of a summery painting to stir up memories of childhood summers of my own.

Above right: Another way to show off precious books, especially those that match up by color and subject, is to place them on a little table and stack them up from large to medium to small to small fry.

Opposite: Bookends allow you to exhibit a small collection of special books outside of the confines of a bookshelf. Case in point, five volumes of vintage Western tales by Zane Grey bookended by a sturdy pair of Native Americans. Their book jackets, mostly intact since their publication in the early 1900s, have faded to wistful watercolor shades that match the romance of their titles, such as *Sunset Pass* and *Stairs of Sand*. The purple fez balanced on top of them, is decorated with sparkly beads that spell out "Golden West" above a decorative elk.

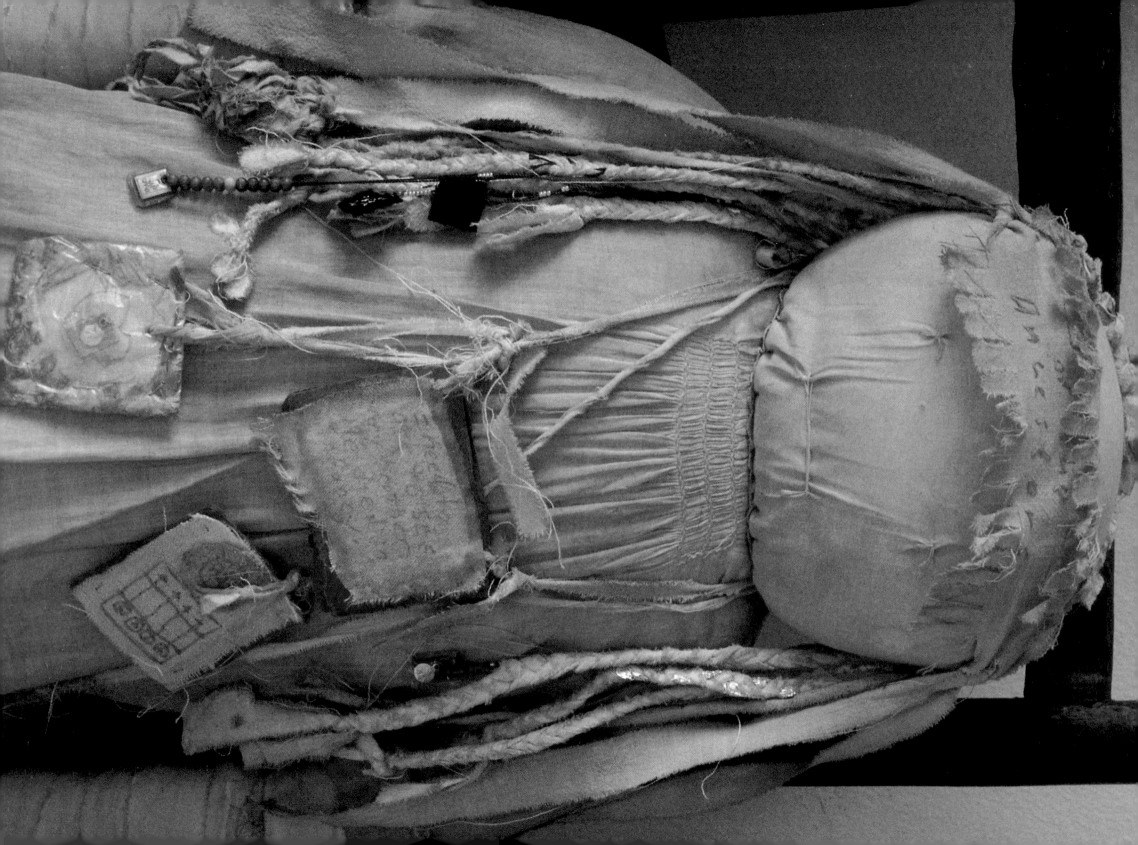

THE OLD RAG DOLL

FRAYED AND FADED, DUSTY AND WORN, AN ARTIST'S CREATION CAN LOOK LIKE A DOLL
BUT CARRY A MUCH BIGGER MESSAGE.

She has sat in an old green ladder-back chair facing our bed for almost twenty years, watching us sleep, recover from fevers, read stories to our children, write books, pay bills, talk on the phone, enjoy an old movie, scratch our dog's chest. Stitched across a cloth band on her forehead is the title the artist Susan McCaslin gave her-Saint of the Ancestors. To me, she is the hippest rag doll ever, with soft Rasta braids intertwined with beads, religious relics, amulets, and tiny totems cascading around her slightly sad yet tranquil face. She is an earth mother dressed in a handmade infant's dress so old that it is almost transparent. Her arms and legs are wrapped with strips of cotton cloth like a mummy. Around her neck, tied together by thin cotton strips, dangle handwritten supplications—"I need to see my brother. He died in infancy"—and embroidered symbols, one of which looks like a primitive calendar. A lengthy, penciled text, hand-written on cloth and sewn onto a small piece of cardboard with dark red thread, reveals the artist's message: "She waits to help us through creating what we expect. She eases the transition from pain to joy, treating us like children, playing our game until we finally accept where we are and who we are and then we can move on." Streaming out of a cotton cavity between her legs are a string of babies, each representing one of life's transitions-"Child to Mother," "Life to Death," "Happy to Sad," "Marriage to Divorce," "Motherhood to Childless," "Child to Adult," 'Failure to Success." She was created as a piece of art, an ancient spirit burdened to intercede for all of us.

Opposite: Sitting in the green ladder back chair, my rag doll saint is a life size thirty-six inches long. Her old smocked baby's dress, once pristine, is now a dusty parchment color as are all her dangling braids, totems and babies.

She waits to help us through, creating what we expect. She eases the transition from pain to joy, treating us like children, playing our game until we finally accept where we are and who we are and then we can move on.

Above: A close-up of the string of cruciform transitional babies each representing one of life's transitions.

Opposite above: The artist's creed, hand-written in pencil and tacked on to a piece of frayed muslin and cardboard, is wrapped in a piece of plastic which has prevented the message from fading.

Opposite, far left: Her muslin braids are intertwined with tiny beads and embroidered patches of felt that resemble religious scapulars.

Opposite left: A tiny religious medal sits in a hand-sewn heart with dried flower petals in the first of three little dangling relics. Above it is a faded handwritten plea, and below is a mysterious symbol stitched over what looks like a calendar.

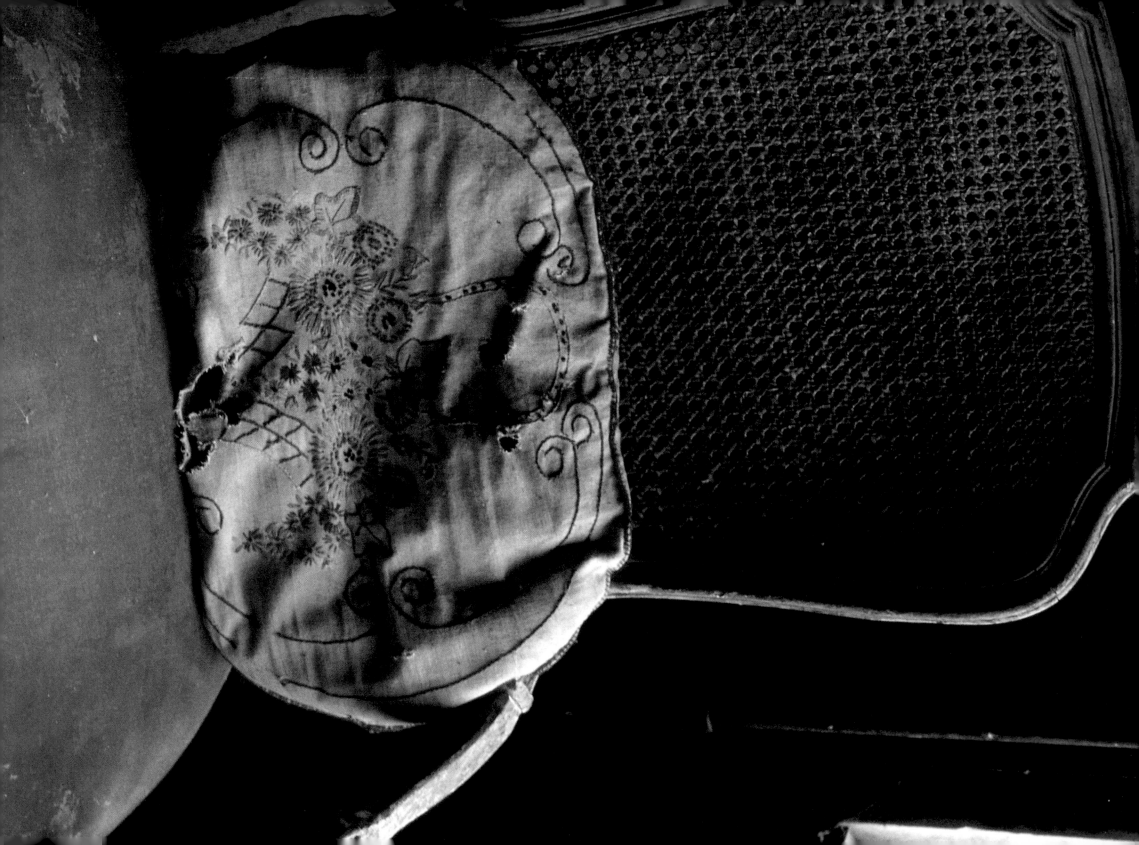

FRAYED AND PATCHED

I have saved this chapter for last—the final act of Old, when the effects of aging cause things to fall apart, unravel, come unglued. Some could say that of me, that I have come unglued to love as I do a pillow, such as the one at left, filled with holes. I admit I can't help myself. When the rain started to seep through the old wooden shingles on the roof of our house in the country, I had to agree to have them replaced, even though they had finally become the way I really liked them, worn and weathered, thick with moss and lichen. I don't like to give up on old things. When my favorite pair of old canvas sneakers were too distressed at heel and toe to wear any longer, I nailed them up on the wall of our barn like an athlete's trophy! I like things that are mended and patched and threadbare, such as ancient Persian rugs that show the boards beneath them and fabrics whose colors have been muted by too much sunlight or cotton blankets softened by too many washings. I love things that are frayed around the edges—old chairs and pillows, hand-made dolls and book covers. Some would say, "They have served their purpose. Get rid of them!" Not me! I say, "Live and let relive—repurpose, recycle, revive!"

Opposite: In the seat of a sort-of Louis XIV gold wicker-backed chair, covered in some indeterminate fabric, touched up with a shade of Pepto-Bismol pink paint, rests a time-tested linen throw pillow; it is decorated with a cross-stitched basket brimming over with wildflowers and an unfortunate collection of holes. It is hard to surmise the origin of the latter. Most likely some little mouse in search of a soft layer for her nest is to blame. I plan (someday) to repair these gaps with patches of old fabrics from my larder of other victims of age and/or circumstance.

Those thrifty early American women who saved every scrap of fabric to patch their family's worn clothing or to create patchwork quilts to warm their beds would chuckle to see glamorous models sporting expensive patched jeans in today's trendy fashion magazines! They would be astonished as well to see their handiwork on display not only in folk art and craft museums but at the Whitney Museum of American Art, which devoted a whole gallery to the quilts of Gee's Bend, a small community in Alabama. My collection will never make it into a museum, mostly because instead of preserving my old quilts, I have constantly used them and have seen them slowly disintegrate. Some loved remnants I have turned into seat cushions to soften the bottoms of old chairs, and others have been turned into decorative pillows to cheer the backs of chairs and benches. Unfortunately, I learned the hard way that old patchwork is more useful to cover a bed than to be sat upon. Before long all that fidgeting loosens stitches and wears away already worn-away fabrics.

Above left: I have softened the seat of a favorite old wicker armchair with a folded-up cotton patchwork quilt that's no longer a worthy bed covering after the demise of many of its patches. Both it and the pillow paired with it have been softly faded by their sunny position in a corner of our country bedroom.

Above right: "Crazy quilts" were made of patches sewn together helter-skelter with no real rhyme or reason to their pattern. This saggy old pillow, hodge-podged out of satin, velvet, and cotton scraps, is obviously kissing kin to this craziness.

Opposite: A set of four bright-green captain's chairs, including the one seen at right, congregate around a wobbly makeshift dining table. I chose them for their sturdiness rather than for their comfort, which is why I am constantly plying their hard seats and rigid backs with disparate pillows. A crazy quilt pillow whose random patches are accentuated with bright blue stitchery affords a little handmade comfort for the sitter.

Most people camouflage the age spots of an old sofa by layering it with coverlets and pillows and the like. Although I have often used this method, I suggest it as a perfect remedy for the opposite problem—a sofa that looks too new! Case in point, our old living room sofa. When we finally replaced it with one covered in a subtle (I thought!) striped ticking fabric, I was astonished at how it stood out. Immediately, I began to layer on old and new textiles from England, Africa, and India. In the corners I nestled a collection of scrappy pillows, making a tempting bed for our black Labrador, Charley!

Since old textiles are too fragile to be used as chair cushions, I tend to display the remnants and decorative pillow coverings I collect by throwing them over the back of a chair or the arm of a sofa, often to hide the telltale signs of the furniture's age. Although I am not particularly knowledgeable about antique textiles, I have always loved the coarse linen that was used as the canvas for samplers created by young women in the early days of American life.

There were very few pattern books, so the sampler became a way to store stitches and designs. The souvenir pillow above is one such example. Its needlepoint message hints to the pine tags sewn inside that give it shape and, at one time, its "A Breath from the Forest" scent. I have partnered it with an equally fragile wooden painted chair—a duo in decline positioned in a tight corner of our country living room where no one would venture to recline.

Opposite, above and below: If you come across a beautiful piece of old fabric, not quite big enough to make a pillow or cover a cushion, consider using it as a decorative flourish, as with this amazing old textile remnant slung over the arm of a settee. If it's a 200-year-old document (a fancy term used by textile aficionados for a venerable remnant) like this one, should you treat it differently knowing how rare and special it is? Should you wrap it in tissue and store it out of sight and out of the damaging light, the heat and humidity of the summer, the sticky fingers of perfectly behaved great-grandchildren? And would you then enjoy it more? No and no and no!

Opposite, near left: Very often old pillows are backed with what was thought of as a less desirable fabric in somewhat gaudy colors, as is the case with the purplish flowery one seen monopolizing a wonderfully battered, mustard-colored, velveteen chair. Birds of a feather flank it—to the left, one of exotic proportions exhibited on a wooden screen, facing a more regularly proportioned cardinal perched outside a slightly misplaced birdhouse.

You climb a twisting stairway of old wooden steps past weathered walls of board and plaster hung with parchment maps of Virginia and England and faded prints of pansies and violets to a narrow landing cozied with shelves of faded books by Vita Sackville-West, Isak Dinesen, Sigrid Undset, and Beverly Nichols, to name a few. Taking a turn to the right and pushing open a pair of wooden panels (an old door cut in two), you enter a bedroom tucked under the sloping roofline. There is a huge window of at least fifty separate panes that fills the room with sunlight and allows a splendid view of the Rappahannock River where the land rolls down to meet it. In the corner is a chair that has over the years been piled with various family member's clothing and personal effects. I don't think it is a chair that is often sat in, and with good reason, because of its dilapidated condition—the tattered fringe, the occasional hole, the shredded strings hanging from the worn-away armrests. My mother has forgotten when or where she got it. No matter. It is safe to say it has lived a good, long life in this most romantic bedroom, keeping watch over the family that has sought rest and shelter in the bed it faces, between two dormered windows, from year to year, from season to season.

Above right: In the country, you can return to the simple pleasures for an evening's entertainment. An old cloth bag filled with children's wooden blocks dangles from the latch of the chipped green cupboard brimming with bedtime reading. The little bag's charming flowered pattern is almost totally camouflaged by the aged brown color of the background fabric.

Opposite: To add character to floors that aren't in great condition, I scatter a few special rugs here and there. Little rugs either hooked, braided, or made of old rags were originally created to warm the chill of floors in early houses heated by fireplaces, and, eventually, became like samplers—a way for the creator to express herself and her adeptness with a needle. Really collectable rugs, in good condition and offering a unique pictorial theme, are often framed and hung like paintings. If you prefer to keep them underfoot, choose a less-trafficked area, and lay them down on a thin rubber pad. A vacumn cleaner can suck the life out of these fragile creations—literally—so when you must, just give them a gentle sweep with an old-fashioned broom. One of my favorite tips, offered by some fanatic old rug lover, was to lie your vintage rugs out in a fresh snow and cover with with a layer of frosty flakes, and then sweep them off along with the dirt—a unique dry cleaning method, I'd say!

Cooking Up Old-Looking Fabrics

If you want to create the look of old pillows or upholstery, throw new fabrics into the washing machine a number of times. With each washing, the colours will fade and the fabrics soften. Better yet, lay your fabric out in the yard or on a clothesline and let the sun, wind, and rain weather it out for a week or so. Or do both!

Never give up on something you love. If, like me, you have a fondness for old pillows, don't let a few holes stand in your way. If you can't live with them, consider patching them with swatches of old fabrics such as denim from a pair of worn-out jeans, or use a new piece and throw it in the wash with a little bleach. Take one little tattered, frayed, and faded stool skirted in a faux cotton and add it to any room in your house, and you have something to talk about. This one, seen opposite, patched-together out of a two-foot barrel, fabric, and a pancake cushion, was more than likely a quick attempt at a dainty stool for a dressing table. Over the years it has served me well covering a big paint spatter on the floor of my Junk Master's Atelier with an air of feminine grace and beauty.

The tried and true instant fabric ager is tea-staining, so pour a cup for yourself and one for your pillow!

⊘ Prewash your fabric. It is always a good idea to test the process with one new and one prewashed piece. Soak in tea, and time the results.

⊘ If you're doing a small piece, add hot water to a very large soup pot. For larger quantities use the hot water setting on the washing machine.

⊘ Add 3-5 teabags to the pot or 5-10 to the washer. Steep a few minutes.

⊘ Add fabric to the tea. Fully immerse and stir to get all areas soaked.

⊘ Check the fabric every 10 minutes or so. For a faint tea-stained look, soak for as little as 20 minutes. For a deep-stained look, soak the fabric for as long as four hours or overnight.

⊘ Different tea blends offer different colors-experiment!

⊘ Drain the tea out of the pot or washer, then refill with water to rinse the fabric—do this several times. To clean out your washer, let it run through an entire cycle with a little soap and bleach.

⊘ Hang tea-stained fabrics to dry, or put into the dryer on a low setting.

I love making our bed. There is something so satisfying about smoothing out a clean white cotton sheet on top of the mattress and tucking another on top of it, then layering on a cotton spread and an old coverlet on top of that, and finishing it off with a folded blanket or two or three at the foot. For years I have fantasized about having a bed like those seen in the primitive mountain cottages of Poland or Russia, piled high with layers of feather mattresses, thick duvets, handcrafted quilts, and a tower of pillows. The closest I came to sleeping in one like that was in an old hotel in the Lake District of England. Sliding into a cozy bed onto soft linen sheets weighed down with thick quilts and discovering the warm surprise of a crockery bed warmer was a dream come true that I am always trying to re-create.

Above: I found this old spool bed in some dusty shop and separated the head and footboards, which are identically decorated, so that I might make two beds out of the one. Because old beds tend to be inadequate for the dimensions of modern sleepers, they need some jury-rigging to make them work. The headboard here is actually screwed directly into the wall. The mattress is supported by a standard metal Harvard frame. The red and blue cotton coverlet was handmade by a nomadic tribe in India. The one at the foot, seen in close-up on the opposite page, is vintage American, made of wool appliquéd with chenille stars. Textiles like these are too fragile for everyday use. Think of them as woven art to decorate the foot of a bed or the back of a chair, chaise, sofa, or wall.

Opposite, far right: Old blankets, like old books, create instant warmth. A stack of machine-made Beacon-like blankets from the 1940s decorates the end of a sofa. Pile them up, layer them over the back of a new sofa, clamp them on a rod to curtain a doorway or window, or stretch them like a painted canvas and hang them on a wall.

Opposite, near right: Take an old headboard like this and use it as an artist's canvas for free-form tulips or whatever is your pleasure.

The rescued castoffs of someone else's childhood—dolls, monkeys, or clowns handmade out of remnant fabrics or fashioned from socks with button eyes sewn on, or crocheted with woolly yarn—provoke memories of our own favorite toys that ruled from atop our pillows and warded off bad dreams at night. Meet my number one hand-me-down clown, above, sprawled on a pillow layered with an old tablecloth, resting on a richly colored serape spread flung over an old iron hospital bed. The weathered striped canvas on the little fold-up stool on the floor beside it mimics not only the stripes of the serape, but also the painting next to it. Clown, tablecloth, serape, and canvas stool are all evidence of the diversity and wonder of great old fabrics.

Opposite, clockwise from top left: The memory of my childhood pink rag doll or the sock doll my grandmother made for me comes to mind whenever I spy an old doll that's stained, torn, frayed, patched, or darned! A spiffy monkey doll in a green beanie holds court on a child's bear rocker; a shabby but sweet little blue sock doll greets overnight visitors on the pillows of a guest bed; a very stylish fellow decked out in a blue and white knitted suit and hat, a little worse for wear, stands tall next to a dainty dolly on a bedside table; a close-up of the clown made out of a cotton sock; a pair of silly cotton frogs camped out on the arm of a sofa startle unsuspecting sitters; a crocheted doll in orange, a paper-doll cutout of a little Dutch maiden, a Victorian image of a mother and infant, and other childish mementos tacked onto a bulletin board covered with vintage fabric create a charming 3-D decoration for a child's room.

To protect your books, especially vintage story books and readers, hunt down some vintage fabrics or wash some yards of new gingham with fabric softener, bleach, and a few tea bags. These three little books—*The Cuckoo Clock* and two early children's readers covered in sweet gingham checks and plaid cotton stripes—recall my family's annual fall ritual of covering our new school books to preserve them. However, ours were usually covered in a sturdy brown craft paper sometimes cut from grocery-store bags and did not hold up as well as these fabric covers!

Mystery is a quality I love in people and things. I am often drawn to things that don't give their history away; something that offers no explanations of what it might have been but is loveable just the same, such as the fabric square of frayed flower patches stitched together like a miniature quilt, seen on these pages and decorating the endpapers of this book. My love for these beautiful little stitched-together floral patches is grounded in their simple beauty. I have no idea what they are or where they came from or even from which flea market I scooped them up. They appear to be uniform in size and theme. Maybe they were giveaways in old seed packages? Don't know! Don't care! I just love them the way the person who collected them and sewed them together did.

Above left: Another mysterious touch was the empty space in the center of the patches. I decided to use it as a space to frame the postcard portrait by Julia Margaret Cameron of a lady (a mysterious one, of course!). Try using an old scrap of fabric instead of matte board to frame a favorite image or postcard in a special way.

Above right: I chose to hang my mysterious miniature patchwork in the most romantic of all places—under a window with a view of green mountains. A better idea might be to choose a frame for it backed by acid-free paper. Old fabrics tacked to the wall will eventually stretch and disintegrate.

Opposite: Tattered seems an apt description for fabrics that have been shredded by time and wear like the flag, baseball hat, and blue sneakers celebrated on these pages and officially nominated for the Tattered Hall of Fame. I am quite confident that my flag of Virginia, held fast by books in an upper shelf of our living room, is in great violation of all guidelines of recorded flag etiquette. The abuse of years (at least twenty) of constant sun and breezes have left its

original blue field faded and its silken fabric in tatters. Unless reported, I am resolved to let it wave to the last shred!

Above left: The frayed front edge of my country neighbor's baseball hat always inspired me. We gave it to him, when it was new, as a present one Christmas. A few years later we gave him a new one, and at my request he turned over his worn and weathered beauty to me. It hangs on a post in our barn, right near

the blue sneakers I retired around the same time.

Above right: I have always worn my summer sneakers like flip-flops-no laces and the heel pushed down for easy-in, easy-out access. When the test of time has reduced them from flip-flops to just plain flops, it's time to retire them. Out in the trash? Oh, no, I have nailed them to a beam in my barn as a tattered trophy of sorts!

This little frayed cotton pillow, measuring
about 9 inches square, has been dubbed the
Gertrude pillow in honor of Gertrude Stein
and her famous phrase, "A rose is a rose is a
rose." That was her tribute to "things are
what they are," and is mine to the rose, which
is the embroidered centerpiece of a square
from a larger piece, possibly a baby's quilt.
Nestled for over a decade in the back of a
wicker chair on a summer porch, it has long
survived the climbing roses blooming not
five feet from it. How long it will stay I cannot say, but I will let it bloom where it is,
touched by sunlight and showers and many a
warm back, until the last petal unravels.

THE WEB IN THE WINDOW

SPIDER WEBS CAN RECALL A CLASSIC CHILDHOOD TALE AND SPIN A ROMANCE ALL THEIR OWN.

Webs definitely get a bad rap. They are associated with haunted houses and evil spiders. But *Charlotte's Web*, the E. B. White classic published in 1952, changed all that.

The heroine spider, Charlotte, as you may recall, saved the life of her friend Wilbur the pig, by spinning the words "Some Pig" in her web. E. B. White taught all of us about friendship, and how we, like Wilbur, can misjudge someone by his or her appearance. "Oh, Charlotte," he said. "To think that when I first met you I thought you were cruel and bloodthirsty." Charlotte, Wilbur, and Fern, the little girl who loved them, certainly changed my mind about spiders. After I read it, every spider I confronted was a distant child of Charlotte. I became much less likely to sweep those webs away—and definitely would not if they were inhabited by a busy little grey spider with a black stripe underneath!

An old house like Muskettoe Pointe Farm, with all its ancient wooden rafters, crevices, and corners, was a most suitable home for a big family like ours, and for spiders, too. On a visit a few years back, I discovered the most beautiful web in the window of the bedroom above the kitchen, which used to be my parents' retreat. The spider had ingeniously crafted her little fragile masterpiece between a miniature stone image of *Alice in Wonderland* and a tiny replica of an English cottage. The morning sun had backlit it perfectly, and so I grabbed my camera to secure the spider's work and the moment. Did I sweep it away after that? Well, of course not. Even though Charlotte's descendant was nowhere in sight, the web was a comfort, just as it had been to Wilbur after Charlotte's death.

"A few strands of her old web still hung in the doorway. Every day Wilbur would stand and look at the torn, empty web, and a lump would come to his throat. No one had ever had such a friend—so affectionate, so loyal, and so skillful."
—*Charlotte's Web*